REICH SPEAKS OF FREUD

REICH SPEAKS OF

Wilhelm Reich discusses his work and his relation

EDITED BY MARY HIGGINS AND CHESTER

WITH TRANSLATIONS FROM THE GERMAN BY THERESE POL

FREUD

ship with Sigmund Freud

M. RAPHAEL, M.D.

New York

CONTENTS

EDITORS' PREFACE

The Wilhelm Reich interview, conducted by Kurt R. Eissler, M.D., representing the Sigmund Freud Archives, took place at Orgonon in Rangeley, Maine, on October 18 and 19, 1952. Reich had intended to publish it, but the decision of the editors to do so was more than mere compliance. In our opinion it is an unusually candid document and its publication supplies a long-waited clarification of the relationship between Freud and Reich.

While Reich in many of his writings did refer to this relationship and to the conflict that developed later, the directness and informality of the interview technique has made it possible to elicit the information in a manner that is both simple and concise, and it should have the advantage of placing the reader in a favorable position to determine for himself what was at issue. Those who are unacquainted with the history of this relationship—and, regrettably, most are—have been bombarded with so discarding Freud's *libido* and remained the only one prepared to defend it.

Although he was never politically oriented, Reich was once violently condemned and, at times, even today, continues to be slandered as a communist because he attached so much importance to the impact of society and saw in Marxist doctrine some basis for hope in bringing about an improvement in the human condition. However, practical communism, as it developed in the Soviet Union, because a monster he termed "red fascism"; and this fact, in addition to his own experiences as a physician among the masses, convinced him that human structure, molded by authoritarian institutions, is protoplasmically unable to change.

In another ironic twist, the psychologists of the communist countries, who had previously held Freudian theory in utter disdain, now see, in the elimination of libido, a basis for compatibility with psychoanalysis through kinship with our latter-day adaptationalists. Thus a Czechoslovakian psychiatrist cheerfully asserts, "If it is true that Freudian statements about instincts and instinctual energy are not essential to Freud's work and can be separated from his empirically based generalizations, I do not see any compelling reasons for Marxists to reject Freud." [4]

Reich never failed to appreciate and express his indebtedness to Freud. In retrospect, he viewed their conflict as a link in the chain of scientific development and, therefore, desirable and even necessary. Throughout this interview, Reich strives to show how essential Freud's formulations were for the clarification he himself sought in clinical matters. For example, Freud's formulation of the negative therapeutic reaction enabled Reich

[4] F. Knobloch, M.D., "Marxists Reject Libido Theory," *International Journal of Psychiatry*, Vol. 2, No. 5, Sept. 1966, p. 559.

to focus on the problem and to arrive at a biological explanation which is fully in accord with clinical facts, instead of at the futile death-instinct hypothesis, which Freud himself acknowledged was only a speculation.

Reich's disappointment in Freud, for which there was much justification, never led to "hatred or rejection." Instead, he came to have "a better and higher estimation of Freud's achievement than in those days when I was his worshipful disciple." Even Adler, Jung and Rank are not denied Reich's indebtedness for the inadvertent assistance their theoretical positions provided in his pursuit of a natural scientific basis for the libido theory. (See Reich's letter to Ferenczi, p. 145.)

Freud, on the other hand, with his authority, tended to foster a static, finalistic condition for psychoanalysis. Anyone who opposed him was considered heretical and no longer part of psychoanalysis. This encapsulation of Freudian theory, and the desire to make it socially acceptable, has tended to deprive it of its historical importance as a foundation for the growth and development which should have been expected of psychoanalysis as a science.

It is now evident that the failure of the psychoanalysts to grasp and utilize the libido theory in a practical way, and the fear it aroused in a rigid social order, has led to its scuttling. Freud's later speculations were designed to reassure a world unprepared to accept any responsibility for its implications. The personal insufficiencies of his followers and the authority of Freud himself, who was unwilling or unable to draw the ultimate conclusions from his early remarkable intuition, created a barrier against any further progress toward an effective therapy and, more important, toward a mass prophylaxis of the neuroses.

Freud's own defection in assuming a biological foundation for our authoritarian culture, thereby limiting the usefulness of his theory, and the lack of practical success in the use of psychoanalysis as a therapeutic instrument have simplified the task for those who now seek to eliminate Freud's influence completely. Reich, alone, did not yield. He is, therefore, *persona non grata*— to the biopsychologists because he gave emphasis to sociology; to the sociopsychologists because he emphasized biology.

Speculating and opinionating about the issues of life do not ordinarily constitute a threat to the established order. Consequently, such intellectual pastimes are usually treated with toleration or indifference. Subjecting these issues to scientific scrutiny, however, almost invariably arouses suspicion and distrust, and ridicule is not an infrequent accompaniment. Then, with the disclosure of a vital truth, all the forces of suppression are mobilized to conceal or destroy it. The discovery of the Life Energy encountered these forces in all their virulence. Every step of the process, from its beginning in the orgasm theory to its culmination in the discovery of a ubiquitous energy, met harassment and slander. These familiar instruments of suppression were finally elaborated into wanton book-burning and incarceration, terminating in the death of Reich in a federal prison.

But, as with the discovery of any fundamental truth, the demonstrable fact of the existence of a universal force cannot be shunted aside or suppressed indefinitely. There is certainly no complacency on the part of those hostile forces seeking so desperately to suppress the discovery. Harassment and calumny continue unabated ten years after Reich's death. Nevertheless, his discovery must eventually evoke a demand for a rational appraisal. It will not lend itself indefinitely to the idle exercise of incompetent or frivolous interpretation. Nor will slander much longer serve to undermine serious consideration of the significance of the discovery. It will not be confirmed or rejected on the basis of the biased opinions of psychoanalysts who can claim authority only in matters pertaining to the psyche, nor in the legalistic maneuverings of chemical-oriented food and drug agencies. The validity of the discovery will be established on the basis of the natural scientific study of such seemingly unrelated phenomena as biogenesis, the cancer disease, gravitational attraction, the development of hurricanes and the formation of deserts in the light of the existence of a universal energy.

The relationship of Reich to Freud and psychoanalysis was the vital first step which led to the discovery of the cosmic orgone energy. To capture the historical significance of this relationship is the purpose of this volume.

The interview was originally recorded on magnetic tape and transcribed shortly thereafter. For the purpose of publication, it was deemed necessary at times to relieve the German style of sentence structure and to delete some redundancies and repetitions. The editors are responsible for such minor changes and are confident that, in making them, no interference with meaning has resulted. We have also provided the footnotes and appended a supplement consisting of correspondence with Freud and others, as well as miscellaneous documents pertinent to the material of the interview.

Unfortunately, the expectation that permission to publish Freud's letters to Reich would be granted was shortlived. Ernst Freud, managing director of the Sigmund Freud Copyrights, Ltd., initially expressed interest only in the payment of a royalty, but negotiations were abruptly terminated and permission refused *on the advice of unnamed psychoanalysts*. The editors had

INTRODUCTORY NOTE

Biographies are usually written long after the issues involved have become meaningless, when nobody can do anything about them, when they have become historical, i.e., ossified. Biographies of important men should be written when everybody responsible for good or bad is still alive and responsive. Why should we be so full of regard for privacy in important matters when our newspapers drown us in small scandals every day?

The developments in science and education within the next one hundred years will be decisive in establishing whether this interview will have any meaning whatsoever, or whether the evasion of the issues of babyhood and motherhood will continue to mess up more centuries of human destiny. It is of crucial importance, therefore, that the major, factual parts of the Wilhelm Reich interview on Freud be published now.[1]

Wilhelm Reich, 1954

[1] In the negotiations which preceded the interview and his acceptance of the documents contributed by the Orgone Institute, Dr. Eissler indicated that the Sigmund Freud Archives intended, wherever possible, to prohibit the use of all material deposited therein for at least one hundred years.

PART 1 THE INTERVIEW

1) OCTOBER 18, 1952

DR. EISSLER

Dr. Reich, the question I want to ask you is a very simple one. It is a very comprehensive question, but it is a simple one. I would like to know everything you know about Freud, everything you observed and everything you thought. Even if it is not based on a correct observation, the mere fact that you thought it about Freud would be so important for us to know.

DR. REICH

Well, that is quite a big order. I know a lot about Freud. I would like to start with a basic theoretical difference in the approach of psychoanalysis and my work, not to propagate my work, but to explain how I saw Freud.

Psychoanalysis, as you well know, works with words and unconscious ideas. These are its tools. According to Freud, as I understood him, as he published it, the unconscious can only be brought out as far back as the Wortvorstellungen [verbal ideas] pened. I don't know whether you know that he withdrew from all meetings and congresses in 1924. And he developed his cancer of the jaw at that time. Are you following me?

DR. EISSLER

Sure, yes, yes.

DR. REICH

Now, cancer, in my research—you know that I worked on it—is a disease following emotional resignation—a bio-energetic shrinking, a giving up of hope.[6]

DR. EISSLER

Yes?

DR. REICH

Now that hooks on to Freud: Why did he develop cancer just at that time? Freud began to resign. (If you don't follow, if anything is unclear, please just ask me. Interrupt me and ask freely.) I didn't see it then, and, peculiarly enough, the conflict between us also began about that time.

Now, I want you to believe that it is not my intention to accuse anybody. I no longer have any interest whatsoever in the psychoanalytic movement. I've been completely on my own since about 1930. Some of the people who were involved at that time are now dead. Some are still alive. Some of their misdeeds still go on, are still active in one form or another. I want to add that whatever happened between the International Psychoana-

[6] *The Cancer Biopathy* (New York: Orgone Institute Press, 1948). "Carcinomatous shrinking biopathy" is the term Reich has applied to the process underlying the disease known as cancer, in which he discovered the functional unity of psychic resignation and biopathic shrinking which precede, often by many years, and accompany the appearance of the malignant tumor.

6)   REICH SPEAKS OF FREUD

lytic Association (IPA) and myself, I ascribed, at first, to this person or that person, to the psychoanalytic association, to a betrayal of Freud and psychoanalysis, etc. And all that turned out to be wrong. Do you know what happened at that time?

DR. EISSLER

Only the gross—

DR. REICH

I shall tell you the details. What happened at that time not only happened in the IPA from 1926 to 1934. It has happened all through the ages. It happened in the Christian Church fifteen hundred years ago. It happened in every home on this planet. Now that sounds peculiar, doesn't it? What happened? Do you know the term "pestilent character"?

DR. EISSLER

Yes.

DR. REICH

That means, briefly, the following: There is a peaceful community—whether it be of psychoanalysts or sociologists, or just a community of people like this town of Rangeley.[7] There are two or three people who are sick, emotionally sick, and they begin to stir up trouble.[8] You still follow me?

DR. EISSLER

Yes.

[7] Rangeley, Maine—the location of Reich's home and laboratories from 1945 to 1957.
[8] The Children of the South, by Margaret Anderson (Farrar, Straus and Giroux, 1966), contains a moving description of a recent example of this phenomenon occurring in connection with the sincere efforts of a community in the South to integrate its school.

7) The Interview

Now, these people are very small and insignificant, historically. But, at that time, they weren't insignificant to me or to other psychoanalysts. At that time, they were important because the fight against the development from understanding human nature on the basis of words or associations or unconscious ideas to understanding human nature on the basis of bio-energetic expression, movement, motion, emotion—in essence, the development from symptom analysis to character analysis and to orgone therapy—was fought, not by argument, not by counterevidence, but by slander. By slander, I say!

There was one man, and I have to point him out. He's dead now. He shot himself. That's Paul Federn.[9] There is evidence that in 1924 this man began to "dig" at Freud about me. I didn't know it then. Freud didn't know it. It became clear later on.[1] He was jealous of my success. And the result was that mess in Lucerne. I don't know what has been deposited in the Freud Archives about me—what slander or defamation. But I know it's around. I know who was involved in it. Jones was in it.[2] I

[9] Paul Federn, M.D. (1871-1950), Viennese psychoanalyst and vice president of the Vienna Psychoanalytic Society from 1924 until its dissolution by the Nazis in 1938.

[1] Evidence of Federn's efforts to disturb the relationship between Freud and Reich was clearly revealed by Freud himself in a letter to Reich dated November 22, 1928, in which he told him that Federn had requested Reich's removal as director of the technical seminar. In a later letter from Freud to Reich, October 10, 1930, Federn's malevolent "digging" was again in evidence.

[2] Ernest Jones, M.D. (1879-1958), English psychoanalyst and official biographer of Freud. In his work *The Life and Work of Sigmund Freud*, Vol. 111, p. 191, Jones referred to the International Congress held in Lucerne in August, 1934. "It was on this occasion that Wilhelm Reich *resigned* from the Association. Freud had thought highly of him in his early days, but Reich's *political fanaticism* had led to both personal and scientific estrangement" (Italics: ed.). Jones knew intimately the circumstances of Reich's *expulsion* from the IPA. Yet, in a work of historical importance we can assume that he deliberately falsified the facts when he stated that Reich

know that. And it is evident from the letters which I wrote to Freud[3] and Freud wrote to me. I don't know if you went through them. Did you read them?

DR. EISSLER

Yes.

DR. REICH

Then you saw it was a great worry. In one letter, Freud expressed his assurance that no matter what people said about me, he would protect me. I don't know if you remember. That was about 1928 or so.[4]

Now, this whole horrible thing burst out at the Lucerne Congress. Do you want to hear about that?

DR. EISSLER

Yes.

DR. REICH

That I seduced all my patients. I was a psychopath. I was this. I was that. Then, finally, I had gone schizophrenic. That went on for years. You know that?

DR. EISSLER

No, I did not know that.

---

resigned. Involved, of course, was the desire to minimize the importance of this event and to absolve the IPA of all responsibility. See Documentary Supplement, p. 255.

Concerning Reich's "political fanaticism," it should be made clear to the reader that the IPA, in order to avoid the implications of the psychoanalytic therapy of the neuroses, sought to discredit Reich's effort to establish the significance of society in the etiology of the neuroses by referring to it as "political fanaticism."

[3] See letter from Reich to Freud, p. 153.

[4] In a letter dated July 27, 1927, Freud assured Reich that, while he was aware of personal differences and hostilities in the psychoanalytic organization, they could not influence his high regard for Reich's competence which, he added, was shared by many others.

seducing patients—the defamation, sexual defamation, and so on. Now, I have to go back to where Freud was in despair.

At that time, about 1925, the psychoanalysts in the technical seminar didn't like my work on genitality, on orgastic potency, on the actual stasis neurosis which underlies the whole dynamic structure of the energy source of the neurosis.[1] And their dislike showed itself in many ways.[2] It would be petty to go into it here and to try to describe these petty ways, petty annoyances, and so on, but I have to say the following: The psychoanalysts didn't like it, and they still don't like it. They don't mention it. It is mentioned nowhere. Genitality, to this day, is not handled as a basic problem of adolescence, as a basic problem of the first puberty. To my knowledge, nobody dares touch it.[3] You'll have to agree with me on that. Nobody dared to touch it then, either. I touched it fully. I went into it critically, as I described it in my *Funktion des Orgasmus*.[4] Do you know that book?

DR. EISSLER

Yes, sure.

[1] "I must repeat what I have said in other publications, that these psychoneuroses, as far as my experience goes, are based on sexual-instinct motive powers. I do not mean that the energy of the sexual impulse merely contributes to the forces supporting the morbid manifestations (symptoms), but I wish distinctly to maintain that this supplies the only constant and the most important source of energy in the neurosis . . ." Sigmund Freud, *Three Contributions to the Theory of Sex* (New York: E. P. Dutton, 1962), pp. 26-7. Originally published as *Drei Abhandlungen zur Sexualtheorie* (Leipzig and Vienna: Verlag Franz Deuticke, 1905).
[2] See letter from Reich to Federn, p. 148.
[3] See statement regarding "Freud, Reich, Kinsey," p. 283.
[4] This book, published in 1927 by the Internationaler Psychoanalytischer Verlag, is not to be confused with Reich's later work of the same title. The early work was dedicated to Freud, and in a letter to Reich dated July 9, 1926, he acknowledged its value, particularly because it dealt with the subject of the actual neurosis.

At first, I didn't understand why that animosity arose. I was regarded very highly from 1920 up to about 1925 or 1926. And then I felt that animosity. I had touched on something painful —genitality. They didn't like it. They didn't want it. Hitschmann[5] was the only one who said, "You hit the nail on the head." (He was the director of the Psychoanalytic Polyclinic. We built it up together.) It is very unpleasant to bring this forth, but I must. It has to do with my plight, and it has to do with Freud's despair.

Basically, Freud discovered the principle of energy functioning of the psychic apparatus. *The energy-functioning principle.* This was what distinguished him from all other psychologists. Not so much the discovery of the unconscious. The unconscious, the theory of the unconscious, was, to my mind, a consequence of a principle he introduced into psychology. That was the principle, the natural scientific principle, of energy—the "libido theory." [6] You know that today very little is left of it.[7] I

[5] Eduard Hitschmann, M.D., joined the Vienna Psychoanalytic Society in 1905 and was the director of the psychoanalytic clinic in Vienna from 1923 until its dissolution by the Nazis. He "always advocated searching for 'organic factors' as a background of the neurosis"—quotation from *Minutes of the Vienna Psychoanalytic Society*, Vol. 1: 1906-1908, edited by Herman Nunberg and Ernst Federn (New York: International Universities Press, Inc., 1962), p. 42.

[6] "We have laid down the concept of *libido* as that of a force of variable quantity which has the capacity of measuring processes and transformations in the spheres of sexual excitement. This libido we distinguished from the energy which is to be generally adjudged to the psychic processes with reference to its special origin, and thus we attribute to it also a qualitative character. In separating libidinous from other psychic energy we give expression to the assumption that the sexual processes of the organism are differentiated from the nutritional processes through a special chemism." Sigmund Freud, *Three Contributions to the Theory of Sex*, pp. 74-75.

[7] None of the present-day schools of psychology utilize the libido theory. Any attempt to revive it is considered naïve and is ridiculed. "Bieber is of

name "Modju" will stick to him for the rest of this century and far beyond. Modju is a scoundrel and—

DR. EISSLER
From where did you derive the name?

DR. REICH
Pardon?

DR. EISSLER
From where did you get the name?

DR. REICH
It was derived from Mocenigo, a nincompoop, a nobody, who delivered a very great scientist, in the sixteenth century, to the Inquisition. That scientist was Giordano Bruno. He was imprisoned for eight years and then burned at the stake. This Mocenigo was a nobody who knew nothing, learned nothing, couldn't learn anything. He wanted to get a good memory function from Bruno, who had a marvelous memory. But he couldn't do it. Bruno couldn't give it to him. So what did he do? He went out and killed Bruno. You see? That's MO-cenigo. And DJU is Djugashvili. That's Stalin.[2] So I put it together to make "Modju." And that is going to stick. They will never get rid of it. Never! That has to do with our present plight in sociology, you understand.[3]

Now, to get back to Freud's despair. As I said, there was this first despair after he discovered infantile sexuality. He was moving quite logically in the direction of the genitality problem, where I found myself so much later, about fifteen years later. But he couldn't get at it. He tried to get at it in the *Three*

[2] Stalin's real name was Josef Vissarionovich Djugashvilli, or Dzhugashvili.
[3] See excerpt from "Truth versus Modju," p. 276.

Contributions. But there, already, something came in which was no good. That was that genitality was "in the service of procreation." That's in the *Three Contributions*.[4] It's not true, you see. He knew it somewhere. In our discussions, it was quite clear that he was hampered by the world, which did not want him to get at the genitality of infants and children and adolescents because that would turn the whole world upside down. Yes, Freud knew that. But he couldn't get at it socially. The sublimation theory,[5] which he developed as an absolute, was a consequence of that. It was an evasion.[6] He had to. He was tragically caught. You know with whom? With the many students, many pupils, many followers. And what did they do? They took what he had and got the money out of it. I'm sorry to have to state that. I stated it publicly before. They hampered Freud. He was hampered so that he couldn't develop further. And from there, he went right into the death-instinct theory.[7] I don't know if you want to go into such detail.

DR. EISSLER

Sure.

DR. REICH

You want it?

[4] "The sexual impulse now [with the beginning of puberty] enters into the service of the function of propagation; it becomes, so to say, altruistic." Sigmund Freud, *Three Contributions to the Theory of Sex*, p. 66.
[5] "The third issue in normal constitutional dispositions is made possible by the process of 'sublimation,' through which the powerful excitations from individual sources of sexuality are discharged and utilized in other spheres, so that a considerable increase of psychic capacity results from an in itself dangerous predisposition." Ibid., p. 94.
[6] "Sublimation, as the essential cultural achievement of the psychic apparatus, is possible only in the absence of sexual repression; in the adult it applies only to the *pregenital*, but not to the *genital* impulses." Reich, *The Sexual Revolution* (New York: The Noonday Press, 1962), p. 19.
[7] See excerpt from *The Function of the Orgasm*, p. 248.

DR. EISSLER

I think so.

DR. REICH

Okay. Freud and I never spoke to each other about personal things. But he was very unhappily married. You know that?

DR. EISSLER

No, I didn't.

DR. REICH

You didn't know that? I don't think his life was happy. He lived a very calm, quiet, decent family life, but there is little doubt that he was very much dissatisfied genitally. Both his resignation and his cancer were evidence of that. Freud had to give up, as a person. He had to give up his personal pleasures, his personal delights, in his middle years. Before that, I don't know. While he had great understanding for what youth is and for what people lived, he, himself, had to give up.[8] Now, if my theory is correct, if my view of cancer is correct, you just give up, you resign—and, then, you shrink. It is quite understandable why he developed his epulis.[9] He smoked very much, very much.[1] I al-

---

[8] "In a manuscript accompanying a letter to Fliess dated May 31, 1897, he laid down the formula: 'Civilization consists in progressive renunciation. Contrariwise the superman.' This is a theme that plays a central part in his later writings on sociology. It probably dates from early life when he was impelled by deep inner motives to renounce personal (sexual) pleasure, and compelled for economic reasons to renounce other enjoyments, with the compensation of achieving thereby intellectual development and interests." Ernest Jones, *The Life and Work of Sigmund Freud*, Vol. 3 (New York: Basic Books, 1957), p. 335.

[9] The term "epulis" is used here by Reich as synonymous with cancer of the jaw. Technically speaking, Freud's cancer was a malignant epithelioma which developed from a leukoplakia, whereas an epulis is actually an inflammatory granuloma and is not malignant.

[1] "All day, from breakfast until he went to sleep, Freud smoked practically without pause . . . usual quantum was twenty cigars a day. . . . He was so fond of smoking that he was somewhat irritated when men

ways had the feeling he smoked—not nervousness, not nervousness—but because he wanted to say something which never came over his lips. Do you get the point?

DR. EISSLER

Yes.

DR. REICH

As if he had "to bite something down." Now, I don't know whether you are on my line. Bite—a biting-down impulse, swallow something down, never to express it.[2] He was always very polite, "bitingly" polite, sometimes. Do you know what I mean?

DR. EISSLER

Yes.

DR. REICH

"Bitingly." Somehow coldly, but not cruelly. And it was here he developed that cancer. If you bite with a muscle for years and years, the tissue begins to deteriorate, and then cancer develops. Now, that cannot be found in psychoanalytic theory. That comes right out of my work, out of orgonomy.

Freud was unhappy in two ways. First, he was caught with his pupils and his association. He couldn't move any more. And, second, he was caught personally. He couldn't show himself anywhere. He sat at home. He had two friends, I think. One was Rie,[3] and there were perhaps two others. One died later. They

---

around him did not smoke." Hanns Sachs, *Freud, Master and Friend* (Cambridge, Mass.: Harvard University Press, 1944), p. 83.

[2] "Once—and only once—I saw him terribly angry. But the only sign of this anger was a sudden pallor and the way his teeth bit into his cigar." Theodor Reik, *From Thirty Years with Freud* (New York: Farrar and Rinehart, 1940), p. 7.

[3] Oskar Rie, M.D., Viennese pediatrician and author, with Freud, of "Clinical Study on Cerebral Paralysis of Children."

in Freud when I offered my assistance to the Freud Archives. It was not interest in the psychoanalytic movement either. I have no interest whatsoever in it. It was not interest in psychoanalytic theory. It was interest in only one thing: How the public institutions will behave in the face of my development of the libido theory; i.e., how they will behave in the face of the biosexual energy development of infants, mothers, pregnant mothers, children in the first puberty and second puberty. I may be wrong. I may be completely cockeyed. I don't think I am. But I assure you that there is no solution to this world's problems unless this point is cleared up sociologically, politically, economically, psychologically, structurally, characterologically, in every single respect. *I don't believe that there will be any solution of any social problem as long as children and adolescents grow up with a stasis of biological energy*—haywire, irrational, with neurotic symptoms, and so on, and so on. That is why I offered my help. Do you understand? Is it quite clear why I'm interested? I have a great interest in getting this point of view into the psychoanalytic movement, in opposition to such schools as the English school, which denies all these things, sees nothing of it, and still thrives on a culture which just falls apart, or is in the process of falling apart, right now, under the very feet of those who proclaim it.

Now, to continue with the basic problem of Freud, Freud as a trail breaker: I said before that he succeeded very well in penetrating to the borderline where language develops, about the beginning of the third year. And, then, he got stuck. Character analysis continued from there. Then, I went on to the bodily expression, which is wordless.[2] I went even further and reached

____

[2] "The concepts of traditional psychology and depth psychology are bound up with *word* formations. The living, however, functions beyond all verbal

the stage where the newborn infant is formed in the womb. Psychoanalysis knows nothing about this. It can't know. That's not a reproach. I don't mean to say that psychoanalysis is bad or insufficient. I say it's a psychology. And psychology has to stick to psychology, to psychological work and ideas.[3] My work continues into the bio-energetic emotional expression. Now, why do I bring this up? I bring it up for a simple reason: If Freud had not existed and done his work, it would not have been possible to penetrate beyond the word language, beyond the unconscious into the bio-energetic expression, into the bio-energetic form of expression of the organism. Then, we wouldn't have learned the following, which no psychoanalyst knows today. You remember the role the so-called "negative therapeutic reaction" played in psychoanalysis. The more you knew, the worse you got. And nobody understood it. Nobody! I began to understand it a few years ago. I would like to try to condense it into a few words.

When a child is born, it comes out of a warm uterus, 37 degrees centigrade, into about 18 or 20 degrees centigrade. That's bad enough. The shock of birth . . . bad enough. But it could survive that if the following didn't happen. As it comes out, it is picked up by the legs and slapped on the buttocks. The first greeting is a slap. The next greeting: Take it away from the

---

ideas and concepts. Verbal language is a biological form of expression on a high level of development. It is by no means an indispensable attribute of the living, for the living functions long before there is a verbal language. Depth psychology, therefore, operates with a function of recent origin. Many animals express themselves by sounds. But the living functions beyond and before any sound formation as a form of expression." Reich, *Character Analysis*, p. 360.

[3] "I have no inclination at all to keep the domain of the psychological floating, as it were, in the air, without any organic foundation. But I have no knowledge, neither theoretically nor therapeutically, beyond that conviction, so I have to conduct myself as if I had only the psychological before me." Sigmund Freud. The quotation appears in Ernest Jones, *The Life and Work of Sigmund Freud*, Vol. 1, p. 395.

Now, may I hook on to the situation as it exists in the world today. How is it understandable that a single Hitler or a single Djugashvili can control eight hundred million people? How is it possible? That was the question I introduced into sociology in 1927. And I discussed the whole thing with Freud. How is it possible? Nobody asks that question. You don't hear about it. *How is it possible that eight hundred million grown-up, hardworking, decent people can be subjugated by a single Modju?* The answer is this—and it's quite sure and safe, and in a hundred years people will know it, I hope—because *infants are ruined in their emotional wanting, in their natural, emotional life expression right before their birth and after their birth.* They are ruined before their birth by cold, by what we call "anorgonotic," i.e., biologically dead, contracted uteri. We have established this in many case histories. Psychoanalysts don't want to know anything about it. They don't listen. The world already listens, however.[6] Can you follow me?

DR. EISSLER

Sure. Yes.

DR. REICH

That means: *The biological system of the human race has been ruined for ages.* It has been ruined for thousands of years in Asia—in China, in Japan. The hardened structures in India and Arabia. The helplessness of millions. That is why the Moscow Modju[7] has such success in Asia. It is also true, of course, in Europe and in America. Everywhere. That means: You break the

6 Numerous articles in popular magazines express this theme of the original and permanent damage to this plastic bit of protoplasm, the newborn.
7 Reich often referred to the pestilent character on the international scene as the "Moscow Modju," the implication being that in the U.S.S.R., in the twentieth century, the emotional plague has achieved its highest and most efficient level of organization. See "Truth versus Modju," p. 276.

will of the infant, of the child. Not when it is in the oedipus phase. That's a consequence. That's later. No, before it's born and soon after, in the first two weeks of life. And, then, the child withdraws. It resigns with a big "NO." It doesn't say, "No." It doesn't scream, "No." But there is an expression of "No." It's a giving up. You can see it in the hospitals. There's no doubt about it. The damage is being done right there, in the very beginning—right before and after birth. *There* is the disposition for all the rest of it. The NO, the spiting, the not wanting, the having no opinion, not being able to develop anything. People are dull. They are dull, dead, uninterested. And, then, they develop their pseudo-contacts, fake pleasures, fake intelligence, superficial things, the wars, and so on. That goes very far. I don't want to go into any more, here. But was I clear now, quite clear?

DR. EISSLER

Yes.

DR. REICH

Now, that is quite crucial, quite crucial. Unless medicine, education, social hygiene succeed in establishing such a bio-energetic functioning in the mass of the population that the uteri will not be contracted, that the embryos will grow in well-functioning bodies, that the nipples will not be contracted, and the breasts of the mothers will be bio-energetically and sexually alive, nothing will change. As long as children will be harmed and hurt with all kinds of ugly things—with chemicals by the chemistry Modju, with injections of all kinds of things, and with the knife right after birth—nothing will change. I have had much medical experience in that. I have pulled many a child out of that mire. As long as that is going on, nothing will happen in the right direction. Nothing! No constitution, no parliament, nothing will help. Nothing, I say. Nothing will change for the better. *You can't impose freedom on the ruined bio-energetic systems of children.* Is this thing clear now? Is this whole thing clear—the impact of the world, as it is, on the infant, yet unborn and newly born? This is the utmost" outpost in biopsychiatry today, the last thing that has been reached. I don't think you can go further in psychiatry than to the period where the infant is in the womb and, then, leaves the womb. Now this has been the major conquest in psychiatry between about 1942 and 1950. It was achieved in psychiatric orgonomy. However, if Freud hadn't existed, if he hadn't found the unconscious, the theory of the instincts, the pregenital development of the child, I couldn't have gone on into the bio-energetic realm, to these things which I have just brought up.

DR. EISSLER

Now, how far were you at the time when this break occurred between you and Freud? How much of these thoughts did you tell him?

DR. REICH

We often spoke about the possibilities of penetrating beyond the association technique.

Then there was the problem of mental hygiene. I want you to understand that, at that time, there was no preventive mental hygiene of the neuroses.

DR. EISSLER

Yes.

DR. REICH

Before 1927, there was nothing of it in our present-day sense—

nothing.[8] So we had to grope our way. And when, in 1927, I established the mental hygiene movement in Austria, I had many meetings with Freud. He was very enthusiastic. And I would like to say that what you know today as psycho-sociology grew out of those discussions.

One day, Freud said (I remember that quite distinctly—it was in connection with the sexual legislation in Russia):[9] "Möglich, dass das Licht vom Osten kommt"—Maybe the light will come from the East. But he was doubtful. I was doubtful, too. I never believed that the communists really were on the right track. But you had to work with them because they had the desolate people.[1] And you had to bring psychological thinking into sociology. Freud was very much in favor of the new legislation in Russia, although he was a bit hesitant about the easing of divorce and its effect on the family. It was quite clear

[8] "There was no talk anywhere of adolescent genitality. One spoke with great dignity of 'Cultural Puberty'; one meant complete genital abstinence during the years of adolescence. . . . There was no sexological institute in Vienna as yet. The Berlin Institute of Sexology under Hirschfeld was mainly concerned with the *legal* affairs of sexology, treatment of perversions in the courts, etc. The Marcuse Institute of Sexology was openminded, but the views of hereditary ethics, not science, governed the scene." Reich, 1952. From the Archives of the Orgone Institute.
[9] The reader is referred to Part II of *The Sexual Revolution* by Wilhelm Reich.
[1] Reich's connection with the communist movement in the late 1920's, which has been repeatedly exploited to discredit him, arose simply from the fact that it was expedient, in order to carry on his work in sexual hygiene, to encounter the masses of the people in a semblance of organization in the socialist and communist parties. Thus, "It was necessary to carry on sex-economic hygiene work within the framework of the socialist and communist parties because that was where the masses of people were at that time. Their problems had to be handled in their life set-up if one wanted to get out of the rut of individual treatment. Furthermore, the physicians who would aid in such matters as birth control, and other aspects of sexual hygiene were in the socialist and communist parties, because Russia, at that time, was still connected with sex-affirmative legislation." Reich, 1952. From the Archives of the Orgone Institute.

there is no curriculum of sexology in the medical school whatsoever, that my colleagues and I want to correct such a situation.
We wanted his help, and he was very ready to give it. He knelt
down before his bookshelf and brought out "Trieb-Schicksale"
and "Das Unbewusste," * and all those things. And he talked a
long time about it and was very much alive. He was very interested. He said, "Finally. It's time." He said it's very important
to have a seminar.

DR. EISSLER

Do you remember some literal statements of his at this first
meeting?

DR. REICH

He said what I told you: "It's very important. It's crucial to
have it. Yes, you are right. It's a neglected subject."

DR. EISSLER

And, then, you started this seminar?

DR. REICH

No, we already had the seminar. The seminar started in January
1919.

DR. EISSLER

That was within the psychoanalytic society?

DR. REICH

No, no! It had nothing to do with it. That was at the University
of Vienna.[1]

---

* "The Vicissitudes of Instincts" and "The Unconscious."
[1] Reich attended the Medical School of the University of Vienna from
1918 until 1922.

DR. EISSLER

And, then, what were your later contacts with analysis? How did you get that?

DR. REICH

Well, I began to analyze.[2] I had my first analytic patient when I was in my third semester, March 1919, I think. I described it in my book on *The Discovery of the Orgone,* in the first volume, *The Function of the Orgasm.*[3]

DR. EISSLER

And when did you see Freud again?

DR. REICH

Oh, I went to see him every once in a while—not regularly, but when I needed something. I still have the cards he gave to patients he referred to me. For example, he would write, "Impotence, three months." Can you imagine trying to accomplish this in three months, or even in six months?

[Change of tape. Dialogue lost.]

I would like to go back to a point which I have here in my notes—Freud's disappointment in me. Now, if there is a disappointment, there must have been an expectation, right? When I first met Freud, there was immediate contact—immediate contact of two organisms, an aliveness, interest, and going to the point. I had the same experience with Einstein when I met him in 1940.[4] There are certain people who click, just click in their emotional contact. You know *Character Analysis* well enough to

[2] At that time, a psychoanalyst was not required to undergo analysis as a prerequisite for the use of this technique in treatment. The rule for a training analysis was adopted later, at the Congress in 1926.
[3] *The Function of the Orgasm,* p. 14.
[4] Reich met Professor Albert Einstein on January 13, 1941. The basis for the meeting and their ensuing correspondence is contained in *The Einstein Affair* (Orgone Institute Press, 1953).

to Annie Angel, a friend of Anna Freud's, that I was the "best head in the Association." The best head, "der beste Kopf." He often expressed the hope that I would continue clinical work, just clinical work. I was a clinician. We agreed that speculations had no meaning. It was easy to put up a theory about a case. I, however, appealed to facts, to the development of the case. And that's what Freud loved. So he had great hopes.

Then I brought in the idea of the technical seminar. It was the first of its kind in the history of psychoanalysis. Hitschmann conducted it first. Then, Nunberg took over, and I followed in 1924. It was really the birthplace of the psychoanalytic technique as it is practiced today. So Freud saw developments, clinical developments. He saw theoretical developments, too. And it was a very great thing to him that life came into that dead body.

Then it happened. I encountered two things in the technical seminar: On the one hand, the clinical situation—the stasis neurosis, the infants, the misery of people. And, on the other hand, the reluctance of the psychoanalysts to go into it—a reluctance that persists to this day. They are still reluctant to go into the problem of stasis neurosis. You get me?

DR. EISSLER

Yes.

DR. REICH

Now that drove me away from the psychoanalytic association— not from psychoanalysis, but from the association, from my colleagues. It drove me into the world outside, into sociology. From now onward, the great question was: *"Where does that misery come from?"* And, here, the trouble began. While Freud developed his death-instinct theory which said "the misery comes from inside," I went out, out where the people were. From 1927 until about September 1930, I worked outside and did all that sociological work at the roots of society. Here, Freud's disappointment comes in. I went into sociology, which, at that time, was mixed or identical with politics. It was one thing. And, here, there was another man, another genius, Marx. I began to be interested in Marx and Engels in 1927. I had to, of course. They were very great men and they all were right. I learned some good, true sociology, there.

Freud was enthusiastic at first—up to about 1928. I remember I visited him on the Semmering, and we had discussions about the mental-hygiene movement. But, then, as it grew, the political side of it, the sociological, took over more and more. And Freud disliked that. Also, Paul Federn had been digging at Freud about me and, about 1929, he succeeded in destroying the splendid relationship between Freud and me with some slander. I don't know what kind of slander. I don't know what went on, but there is no doubt that it was Federn who kept digging at Freud about me. He dug and dug and dug—probably as far back as 1923. And, then, when the sociological work developed outside, Freud began to yield. *I had drawn the social consequences of the libido theory. To Freud's mind, this was the worst thing I did.*[9]

Now, what are these social consequences? What are the social consequences of the libido theory? You have it in all my publications. I would like to summarize it in a few words: If you have a stream, a natural stream, you must let it stream. If you dam it up somewhere, it goes over the banks. That's all. Now, when the natural streaming of the bio-energy is dammed up, it also spills

[9] "The clash between Wilhelm Reich and Sigmund Freud only reflects the clash of the cultured secure world with the true life of the people at large. This is a frightening chapter of knowledge." Reich, 1952. From the Archives of the Orgone Institute.

over, resulting in irrationality, perversions, neuroses, and so on. What do you have to do to correct this? You must get the stream back into its normal bed and let it flow naturally again. That requires a lot of change in education, in infant upbringing, in family life. These are the social consequences. And, somehow, here, Freud couldn't follow me. It was not the character-analytic technique, it was the sexual revolution[1] that bothered him. Any questions?

DR. EISSLER

What were his objections?

DR. REICH

There were no objections. "Kultur," that's all. I want to have it quite clear that Das Unbehagen in der Kultur[2] was written specifically in response to one of my lectures in Freud's home. I was the one who was "unbehaglich in der Kultur."

DR. EISSLER

There was a discussion? Did Freud discuss that paper? Which paper was the one—

DR. REICH

Yes. My paper was that on "The Prophylaxis of the Neuroses."[3]

DR. EISSLER

Yes. And what did Freud say?

[1] "When I coined the term 'Sexual Revolution' in the 1930's, I had the vision of a basic change from the prevalent negation of life and love to a rational, life-positive, happiness-enhancing handling of the love function of mankind." Reich, 1952. From the Archives of the Orgone Institute.
[2] Freud, Civilization and Its Discontents. The word unbehagen means literally "dis-ease." According to Jones (The Life and Work of Sigmund Freud, Vol. III, p. 48), Freud had originally suggested as the title for this volume "Man's Discomfort in Civilization."
[3] Delivered in Freud's inner circle on December 12, 1929.

Freud's remark was, "Die Kultur geht vor." [4] I say he was irrational. I am sorry. He was irrational. I said to him, "If your own theory says that the stasis, the libido stasis or energy stasis, is at the core of the neurosis, of the neurotic process, and if the orgastic potency, which you don't deny (he never denied that), is a key to overcome that stasis, or, at least, to deal with it, then my theory of the prevention of the neuroses is correct. It's your own theory. I just draw the consequences of it." But he didn't want it. Here, he was the old gentleman, bound down by his family, bound down by his pupils, who were partially neurotic and partially bound down by their families. Hitschmann was one of the few who really understood. [5] The enemies were Nunberg and, especially, Federn. Helene Deutsch was very sympathetic, but noncommittal. Who else? Horney understood, but she dropped the sexual angle. Rado[6] was far off. Alexander was always far off. Yes, Alexander was an enemy. [7] Anna Freud understood. She was always very interested and friendly, but she was also noncommittal.

So, because Freud's expectations had been so great, his disappointment was equally great. He felt that here was a clinician, a psychiatrist, a man trained in natural science, eager, gifted, who could carry on. And then he goes off into Marxism, Communism, and so on.

Now, I can assure you I made many mistakes at that time. For instance, it was a mistake to believe that if you tell the people about a neurosis and if you tell them about happiness, they will

[4] "Culture takes precedence."
[5] See correspondence between Reich and Hitschmann, p. 226.
[6] Sandor Rado (1890-   ), psychoanalyst whose recent work has emphasized "adaptational psychodynamics." See preface.
[7] See excerpt from *The Function of the Orgasm*, p. 248.

DR. EISSLER

Yes.

DR. REICH

That's what I mean, today, when I speak of the "emotional plague." And my knowledge of all this came out of these experiences. You understand?

DR. EISSLER

Yes. Did Freud see the difference between politics and sociology?

DR. REICH

No, no! Nobody knew it then. We had to learn about it through our mistakes. Thus, for instance, we had to find out what those politicians, those communist red fascists,[1] were doing in Berlin in 1931-1932. As long as I brought ten thousand, twenty thousand, forty thousand youths into their organization on the basis of the sexual question and the mental-hygiene question, they said, "Reich is marvelous." The moment it came to doing

_____

long as they saw people streaming into meetings to obtain information and help regarding their private lives, the politicians were all for it. 'Politicians', here, not only means the party politician, but it means every man or woman to whom power, influence, career means everything, and human misery and knowledge nothing.

"As soon as the sex-political question revealed its force, its tremendous social importance and its emotional impact on people, and as soon as the physician, educator, and functionary faced the grave problem of how, practically, to go about the mass misery in the midst of all the ideological, medical, scientific confusion, with thousands of noises babbling and chattering wrong ideas all around them, the politicians again slandered in order to destroy the true issue of the mental and sexual health of the multitudes. Then, having destroyed the issue, or debased it by politicking means, they took over the people for further betrayal. This was typical procedure, and it will occur until there are powerful centers based on knowledge and skill which will be able to cope with this tremendous issue of man." Reich, 1952. From the Archives of the Orgone Institute.
[1] See "Basic Tenets on Red Fascism," p. 274.

something practical, they became enemies. Now, that is crucial. As long as I brought them people, I was "wonderful." The moment they had to do something practical for people, they became hateful. You get me? [2]

DR. EISSLER

Yes.

DR. REICH

The scoundrels! They don't know what to do or how to go about things. And that is why they are politicians. I think they have no worse enemy, today, than me, and they know it. Therefore, they behave the way they do.

DR. EISSLER

What did you suggest?

DR. REICH

It was quite clear. You have to establish youth centers. You have to train many physicians. You have to teach sex economy.[3] You

[2] "While I was accused by Freud of criticizing his psychoanalytic theory on behalf of and at the command of Moscow, Bischoff and Schneider, two Berlin stooges of the Moscow dictators, were using the most intricate devices of defamation, underhandedness, distortion, lies and calumny in order to wrest some fifty thousand men, women, adolescents and children from my influence. These people had joined the Sexpol organizations in Germany solely because I had made them look at social institutions from the standpoint of the gratification of human needs. In contradistinction, the red fascists were only interested in state power and in getting social influence by misusing what I had built up. They were not at all interested in the factual, concrete solution of the sexual misery of people. Therefore, they fought me as an 'anti-Marxist, counter-revolutionary Freudian'. A few years later, I pulled out of this Freudian and Marxian mess and moved onto the road which led to the common functioning principle underlying both Freud's and Marx's discoveries, i.e. the living in the human unconscious mind as well as in the human creative working power." Reich, 1952. From the Archives of the Orgone Institute.

[3] "The orgasm theory and the character-analytic technique both were rejected and never mentioned in his writings by Sigmund Freud. I had to

have to bring human psychology into your politics. You have to do more. You have to revamp your whole way of thinking, so that you don't think from the standpoint of the state and the culture and this or that, but from the standpoint of what people need, what they suffer from. Then, you arrange your social institutions accordingly. Not the other way around.[4] Now, that is foreign to the mind of a Marxist politician today. They only think in terms of "productive forces." They think in terms of the state. I think in terms of human beings and what they need. If I had anything to say politically, everything which exists would be arranged in accordance with what the child needs, the infant needs, the adolescent needs, you need, I need, everybody needs.[5] Now, here, sociology becomes separated from politics for the first time.

So I moved out of psychoanalysis. No, not quite. I was still in psychoanalysis, but I moved into sociology, into the field of human mass action. Then, Freud was disappointed.

---

proceed on my own and called it, from 1928 onward, Sex-Economy." Reich, in a letter to Dr. Eissler, February 19, 1952.

Reich used the word "economy" in its sense of the managing or regulating of functions. Thus, "sex-economy" denotes that knowledge which deals with the economy of the biological energy in the organism, i.e., with the capacity of the organism to regulate or balance its sexual (biological) energy. See also Documentary Supplement, p. 270.

[4] Contrast this with the psychoanalytic position which does not bother to question the origin of the existing social institutions, but treats them as if they are biologically given, and, therefore, proceeds to bring about adjustment to them.

[5] Compare this with Anna Freud:

". . . the child must learn how to conduct itself in regard to its instinctual life, and his [the therapist's] views must in the end determine what part of the infantile sexual impulses must be suppressed or rejected as unemployable in the cultural world." The Psychoanalytical Treatment of Children (New York: Schocken Books, 1964), p. 54.

Also: "In working with an adult we have to confine ourselves entirely to helping him to adapt himself to his environment. It is far from us, and in fact lies quite outside our intention or our means, to shape his surroundings to meet his needs." Ibid., p. 61.

DR. EISSLER

He warned you not to do it?

DR. REICH

No, he didn't. It was Modju Federn who did it.[6] I don't know
what he told Freud about me. I only know that at the Lucerne
Congress he and Jones did all kinds of things. They told people
that I was psychopathic, that I was sleeping with many women,
and so on. Do you understand?

DR. EISSLER

Yes. When did you see Freud personally the last time?

DR. REICH

The last time I saw him was in September 1930, before I went
to Berlin. I visited him in Grundlsee and had a very sharp discussion with him. He was very sharp, and I was very sharp, too.

DR. EISSLER

That was in 1930?

DR. REICH

1930. September. I had just published the first part of *The Sexual Revolution* under the title "Geschlechtsreife, Enthaltsam-
keit, Ehemoral." [7]

DR. EISSLER

Yes. And what was the sharp discussion about?

DR. REICH

It was about the following: I said that you have to distinguish
the natural family, which is based on love, from the compulsory
family. I said you have to do all kinds of things to prevent neu-

[6] See letter from Reich to Federn, April 18, 1933, p. 163.
[7] "Sexual Maturity, Abstinence, Marital Morality."

DR. REICH

No, that was at a meeting. There were about seven or eight psychoanalysts who met at Freud's home, and I was one of them. There was, I think, Hitschmann and Federn, Jekels—I don't know whether Jekels was there.

DR. EISSLER

Probably.

DR. REICH

Yes. I, Nunberg, Deutsch. Maybe Hartmann[4] was there. I don't know. Some were guests. They took turns—some coming one time, some at another. I was among the steady ones. So there I brought forth "Die Prophylaxis der Neurosen." (If you read my *Function*, you will have more of the details.) And there it was already heated. There was a very calm, cold atmosphere, but I insisted: First, *you must shift from therapy to prophylaxis*—prevention. Second, you must concern yourself with the family, which is the origin of the oedipus conflict, and so on. It was cold. They were revolting. Freud was very hard with me, but it was a good hardness. I didn't dislike it.

DR. EISSLER

Yes. But what did he say?

DR. REICH

At that meeting he maintained that it is not the task of psychoanalysis to save the world. He was right.

DR. EISSLER

He thought the world cannot be saved, therefore—

[4] Heinz Hartmann (1894-   ), editor of the *International Journal for Psychoanalysis*, 1932-1941, at present on the faculty of the New York Psychoanalytic Institute.

DR. REICH

Freud was resigned. I tell you he had a cancer in his mouth. He was resigned. He couldn't think differently any more. Besides, he was older. The age itself wouldn't have done it, you understand. It was a characterological resignation, as I described it before.

DR. EISSLER

But he did not think that if there were means of reorganizing the family that it should not be done?

DR. REICH

I don't know. I can't tell. But my impression was that, *here, the Freud of the Victorian era contradicted the Freud who had discovered infantile sexuality.*[5] Here, perhaps, he was bound down personally. And he had had enough. He had had enough struggle. And he was right again. If I had known in 1930 what was awaiting me—slander and defamation from the psychoanalysts, that Lucerne scandal, and all the things that went on in Norway from 1937 to 1939, and, then, here in the United States[6]—I wouldn't have done it. Do you understand?

[5] In a letter to Otto Fenichel dated March 26, 1934 (see documentary Supplement, p. 176), Reich wrote, "The basic debate between dialectical-materialist and bourgeois psychoanalysts will primarily have to prove where Freud the scientist came into conflict with Freud the bourgeois philosopher; where psychoanalytic research corrected the bourgeois concept of culture and where the bourgeois concept of culture hindered and confused scientific research and led it astray. 'Freud against Freud' is the central theme of our criticism."

[6] See documentation of this reference to the attacks upon Reich professionally and personally, p. 230 ff. The responsibility for the instigation and perpetuation of these vicious attacks culminating in Reich's imprisonment and death must be laid at the door of the psychoanalysts. Their attempts to absolve themselves of this responsibility by references to Reich's sanity must be scrutinized in the light of this interview, which was requested and conducted amidst these desperate efforts to discredit and destroy Reich and his work by groundless slander.

DR. EISSLER

Yes.

DR. REICH

I wouldn't have started it. Is that clear? You see, the question is: *Will our children, in a hundred years, when they are five or six years old, be able to live their natural lives as nature or God ordains it? Or will they sublimate according to Anna Freud?* Is that clear now?

DR. EISSLER

Yes.

DR. REICH

That's the problem. If I can help it, the first will be the case. I hope so. *Sublimated work or good cultural achievement is possible only after the basic needs are satisfied.*[7] I already taught that in 1927.

DR. EISSLER

Yes.

DR. REICH

That's all published. I don't have to repeat it here. What's important here is more the personal element in it, i.e., Freud's inhibition due to his own personal structure, his own resignation.*

[7] The term "sublimation" is flagrantly misinterpreted and misused. For example, the importance of the direct gratification of human sexual needs has often been deliberately minimized in an effort to dispose of the problem of what is to become of the sexual energies released from repression during the therapeutic process in the face of the obstacles of a sex-negating society. Sublimation, in its misused sense, is supplied as an inoffensive substitute mechanism. See footnotes 5 and 6, p. 19.

* See the reproduced pages from Reich's marked copy of Volume I of the Jones biography (following p. 142), with his handwritten notations: (left) "Freud was simply love-starved, like a steam engine before explosion"; (right) "Begin. Resig." (Beginning Resignation.)

his being bound up with a family he most probably didn't like. Puner has it in her book.[8] I don't know whether you know the book. Then, there was his organization and the enemies. They only waited to say that he was immoral. That's what they said about me, later.[9] Is that clear? Well, that's about it. Any questions, Doctor? Go ahead.

DR. EISSLER

Do you know anything about his opinions regarding those pupils you mentioned? Or didn't he talk about it at all?

DR. REICH

He talked about it. Yes. Not too much. Well, all right, let's deposit it. Hitschmann once told me that Freud couldn't stand Federn's eyes. He referred to them once as "patricidal eyes." And that was quite true. Wonderful! Federn really had murderous eyes. Yes!

DR. EISSLER

That's the only remark you know about?

DR. REICH

Oh, there are very many others. Yes, it has to come out. Freud knew, of course, of the sexual disturbances. We never really spoke about it, but it was quite obvious that he knew. He despised them very much. He despised his pupils. He referred to them once in the early years as—what was it? Vermin, or what? Yes, he suffered very much from this. He was very biting. He talked ironically. I remember once he got Nunberg going. Freud said, "Now, what you did now is, again, the same thing. You

[8] Helen Walker Puner, *Freud: His Life and His Mind* (Howell, Soskin, 1947).
[9] See letter from T. P. Wolfe, M.D., to the editor of the *Psychiatric Quarterly*, p. 233.

take a bone, like a dog, and you crawl in the corner. You chew
the bone and you think the bone is the world." Yes, he was very
sharp and biting.[1] He was never ironic toward me, but he was
very mad at me.

I wonder how much time we have to work things out. Would
you have had enough, now?

DR. EISSLER

No, I would like to go on.

DR. REICH

What?

DR. EISSLER

I mean, it's your fault that you are speaking in such a fascinating
way that I don't notice the time, really.

DR. REICH

All right. Now, I could go on and on because it is endless. That's
what Freud means to me. Freud is like Columbus who landed
on a shore and opened up a continent. You understand?

Now, Freud had a severe conflict with Judaism. Here, he was
bound down, too. On the one hand, out of protest against the
persecution he had suffered, he maintained very bravely and
very courageously that he was a Jew. But he wasn't. Freud was
not Jewish. Do you know what I mean, now?

DR. EISSLER

Yes.

DR. REICH

To me, as a characterologist, a Jew is somebody who behaves in

[1] "Sigmund Freud had a [sense of] humor which at times was colse to
sarcasm. Such humor serves the protection of the Ego from too great, un-
bearable sorrow." Reich, 1952. From the Archives of the Orgone Institute.

a Jewish way, either nationally or religiously, who is bound up with his customs, who speaks the Jewish language, who lives in it, thrives in it, and so on. Now that is quite crucial. In our character analysis, this plays an important role. For instance, was Roosevelt a "Hollander"? No, he was an American. Right? So Freud was really German. His style, his thinking, his interests, everything was German. And, here, he was torn apart. On the one hand, he was a Zionist. On the other hand, he was a German. He liked Goethe, *Faust*. His language was German. His style was the wounded German style of Thomas Mann—the rounded, harmonic, but very complicated expression, in contradistinction to the English, which is straight and simple. That became more and more apparent in Freud as the years went by and his fame grew.[2] And, then, there was his interest in Moses, who, to Freud's mind, wasn't a Jew either.[3] Is that clear?

DR. EISSLER

Yes.

DR. REICH

To me, that meant that Freud didn't really want to be a Jew. But he couldn't cut loose.

DR. EISSLER

Yes.

[2] See Reich's statement, which accompanied the delivery of his paper "Ibsen's Peer Gynt, Libidokonflikte und Wahngebilde" to the Sigmund Freud Archives, concerning the literary style of Freud and the early psychoanalysts, p.

An interesting parallel, today, is to be found in the stilted, formal, unemotional style of Masters and Johnson in *The Human Sexual Response*, which attempts to deal with socially embarrassing research in the sexual realm.

[3] Sigmund Freud, *Moses and Monotheism* (New York: Vintage Books, 1955).

DR. REICH

And when the Nazis began to persecute, he suffered very much.[4] I think he died because of that. It was not just the cancer. He was done.

DR. EISSLER

Did it [Freud's Judaism] lead to a limitation in thinking?

DR. REICH

No, it led to a sharp contradiction in him. He suffered, just plain suffered from it. He didn't want to be a Jew. Never. He wasn't Jewish. I never felt he was Jewish. Neither did I feel Anna Freud as Jewish. They had nothing Jewish in them, either characterologically, religiously, or nationally. That doesn't mean I'm anti-Semitic.

DR. EISSLER

No, I understand.

DR. REICH

You understand? Now, many Jews have suffered from that. In "Moses," it's clearly expressed. Freud was the Moses who never reached the promised land. His unconscious was only an idea. It's not real. It was never real. You know where it becomes real?

DR. EISSLER

No.

DR. REICH

In the twitchings which we get out of the organism in our work. Do you know anything about it? You don't? The unconscious

4 The obvious implication is that Freud, being and wanting to be German, was tormented by the severe blow to this identification, and the necessity, under the circumstances, to reassert his Jewishness.

comes out in orgone therapy in actions of the protoplasm.[5] He didn't reach that. I think he was a very eager physician. He wanted to cure people, but it didn't work. It just didn't work.[6] So you see, there were many reasons for Freud's resignation.

DR. EISSLER

You remember some actual statements he made about Jews, Judaism, his relationship to it?

DR. REICH

No, I never heard a direct remark, but he used to quote Jewish jokes. He had much contempt in him for people. He made these jokes, but he was not anti-Semitic. Surely not. Much of his Judaism was protest, not genuine. I may be wrong in all this, you understand, but I just give you my impressions. His German was perfect. His thinking was German. It was not Jewish, even thought Janet [7] had proclaimed that psychoanalysis was a Jewish science.

Now, while Freud was caught in Judaism, I was free of it. I'm

[5] Making the unconscious conscious, which is, in essence, the function of psychoanalysis, is a speculative, intuitive process of interpretation. In orgone therapy, the attack upon the characterological and muscular rigidities effects a release of bio-energy which is expressed in clonic movements and the experience of bodily sensations described as streamings. This movement provides an objectively expressive language, eliminating the need for the verbal psychoanalytic speculations condemned by many as unscientific.

[6] "The man who founded the discipline which became the sharpest tool in clinical psychotherapy was himself, in the second half of his life, not particularly enthusiastic about its therapeutic benefits . . . as the years passed he lost interest in psychoanalysis as a means of cure, and became more concerned with its development as a body of theoretical knowledge applicable to the interpretation of cultural phenomena . . . while he formulated the basic therapeutic procedure of psychoanalysis which is still widely used today, he eventually became negligent of the possibilities the procedure offered." Helen Walker Puner, *Freud: His Life and His Mind*, p. 261.

[7] Pierre Janet (1859-1957), French neurologist and psychologist known principally for his investigation of hysteria through the use of hypnosis.

much more in sympathy with the Christian world of thought and the Catholic realm. Not that I condone it, or that I believe in it. I don't believe in these things. But I understand them well. The Christians have the deepest point of view, the cosmic one. The American Jew has it, too, but not the European. I don't know whether we should go into that. But I am very much interested in the history of Christianity. Do you know what Christ knew? He knew about the Life Energy. I don't know if you get me now. In a simple way, he knew about the fields and the grass and growth and babies. That's what he knew. Freud didn't. Freud was anti-emotional, very anti-emotional. Freud was for intellect only, you understand. I myself am quite intellectual. But intellect without an emotional basis can't quite fully live or work.[8] *Now, I know why he was against the emotions. He opposed them because he rejected the secondary emotions, the perverted emotions. And the normal emotions, the natural ones, the deep ones—nobody knew anything about them, then.*[9]

[8] "According to the common view, the function of the human intellect is exclusively objective and directed toward reality; ethics and philosophy, in particular, regard intellectual activity one that comprehends reality 'incorruptibly', and which is absolutely antithetical to the affect. This view overlooks two things: first, the intellectual function is itself a vegetative activity, and second, the intellectual function may have an affect charge no less intensive than that of any purely affective reaction. Character-analytic work, furthermore, reveals a specific defensive function of the intellect. Intellectual activity has often such a structure and direction that it impresses one as an extremely clever apparatus precisely for the *avoidance* of facts, as an activity which really *detracts* from reality. The intellect, then, can work in both of the basic directions of the psychic apparatus, toward the world and away from it; it can work in the same direction as a vivid affect, and it may be in opposition to it. That is, there is no mechanistic, absolute antithetical relationship between intellect and affect but, again, a functional relationship." *Character Analysis*, p. 312.

[9] "The moralistic world has for thousands of years, especially since the beginning of early patriarchy, suppressed the natural genital drives. It has thus created the 'secondary' or perverse and pornographic drives, and was then forced to build up a wall of moralistic, hygienically disastrous laws and rules against the same pornographic human mind which was first created by

DR. EISSLER

Yes. Now in one of your letters you said that you saw Freud at the window like a caged animal.

DR. REICH

That was that September, when we parted.

DR. EISSLER

In Berchtesgarden?

DR. REICH

No, no, in Grundlsee. Oh, that was very tragic, very tragic. We had a discussion. I suggested that to be quite sure that I was right [about the social problem] and that there was not an irrational element in my thinking, I would try to consult with some

---

the suppression of *natural* sexuality." Reich, 1947. From the Archives of the Orgone Institute.

According to the psychoanalytic concept, "the unconscious mind is composed of nothing but asocial drives which, quite logically, *must* be suppressed . . . it does not contain any instincts which are essential for the process of living. All social and cultural attitudes are 'sublimations' of antisocial drives. In short, psychoanalytic theory assumes that the unconscious is the *last* biologically given realm; that there is nothing behind what the analyst can find in the depth of the person. This theory knows nothing of the bio-energetic functions in the core of the living system; neither does it penetrate deeply enough into the realm of bio-energetic functioning to realize that the 'polymorphous perversity' and antisociality of the unconscious are artifacts of our culture which suppresses the naturally given bio-energetic emotions; it does not realize that these artificial, 'secondary drives' (Reich) are constantly fed by frustrated libido.

"This outlook is, of course, quite hopeless as far as the prevention of neuroses is concerned: If the unconscious, antisocial drives are biologically given, if the child is born a 'wild, cruel, asocial animal,' then there is no end in sight for the emotional plague. Children from birth on are conditioned and adapted to the culture based on suppression of the secondary drives. The psychoanalyst sees nothing but thwarted life which he mistakes as the naturally given biology of man. The armoring which takes place from birth onward obfuscates completely the *artificial* nature of what the psychoanalyst sees and describes." Editorial note, Orgone Energy Bulletin, Vol. 2, No. 2 (April 1950).

prominent colleague in Berlin. He told me that since I was the founder of the modern technique in psychoanalysis I would meet with great difficulties. It would be difficult to find somebody to treat me. But he said it would be possible to discuss it on a colleagual basis. I told him, "All right, I shall try." And he suggested either Rado or Bernfeld. I said, "I shall see, yes." I saw Rado several times. Nothing came of that. Rado was very jealous, awfully jealous.

But to return to our last meeting. We talked for about an hour, maybe an hour and a half, and I left. I knew it was the last time I would see him. Somehow, I knew that I wouldn't see him again. I walked down. And as I left, I looked up at his window, and I saw him walk up, down, up, down, fast, up-down, up-down, in that room. I don't know exactly why this impression remained so vivid to me, but I had the impression "caged animal." And that's what he was. Every man of his greatness, of his vivacity, of his spirit, who knew what he wanted and landed where he did would behave like that, like a caged animal. I have a very good feeling for movement and for expressions, and that was my impression—caged animal. I don't know how many psychoanalysts were aware of that. I don't think very many. I don't know.

DR. EISSLER

Before, you mentioned Freud's meanness. That I think would be important.

DR. REICH

Meanness? Did I say that word? Did I use that word?

DR. EISSLER

I thought you did.

Not meanness. Irony, a biting irony. He—how shall I formulate that? I think the following happened: You see, every pioneer has to have friends and co-workers to carry his work. Now, what usually happens is that they are not around, or if they are around, they take advantage of the pioneer. That's a very dreadful truth, but it is truth. He waits and waits and waits for somebody to come around, to help, to do things and to go along with him. But they are just dead. You see, *the pioneer somehow jumps out of the present-day biological structure of humanity. You know that? He jumps out of it because of his aliveness. But humanity sits, sits, just plain sits.*

Oh, yes, I remember a very nice thing. It was at the Congress in Berlin, 1922. I was still very young then. I had only analyzed for about two or three years. There were about one hundred and fifty people there. And Freud and I and a few others were standing together. Freud moved his hand over that crowd and said, "Sehen Sie diese Menge hier?—See that crowd? How many do you think can analyze, can really analyze?" He raised five fingers. That showed he knew. Not that they are bad men or bad physicians, but the real understanding, the real contact, the "feel" as I call it, was missing. Yes, Freud was very much alone. He couldn't associate with any of his students. Why? Because every single one would go at him and hook onto him. He was a daddy. He was the father. He had to give everything. He had to love everybody.[1] The Berliners, for instance, were very proud that

---

[1] "Everybody around Freud wanted to be loved by him, but his intellectual accomplishment meant infinitely more to him than the people around him. As an inspired pathfinder he felt justified in regarding his co-workers as a means towards his own impersonal accomplishment; and with this end in mind, probably every impulse towards originality, when it subserved other than *objective* purposes, annoyed him and made him impatient. Freud was too far ahead of his time to leave much room for anything really new in his

they were not Viennese. You know why? Because they didn't have that infantile attitude toward Freud. But they had it toward Abraham.

Now, about Freud's contempt. I don't think he liked people. Do you know what I mean?

DR. EISSLER
Yes.

DR. REICH
I don't think he liked people. I may be wrong. I don't think so. Oh, of course he liked a few people. I know he liked me, and he liked some others. For example, he liked his daughter very much, and I know he liked Bernfeld for a while. He also liked Abraham very much, but not very personally. He respected him. I know that he liked Ferenczi.[2]

DR. EISSLER
He spoke with you about Ferenczi?

DR. REICH
Oh, we didn't speak as you and I are doing now, sitting here. If I had some problem, I went up, and we talked, half an hour or an hour.

DR. EISSLER
Do you remember what specific problem which you probably—

---

own generation. It seems to be characteristic of every discoverer of genius that his influence on contemporary thought is not only fructifying but inhibitory as well." Helene Deutsch, *The Psychoanalytic Quarterly*, Vol. IX, 1940.

2 "He loved those who were critical, who were independent, who were of interest for their brilliance, who were original." Helene Deutsch, *The Psychoanalytic Quarterly*, Vol. IX, 1940.

Oh, yes, neurasthenia. The neurasthenia problem.[3] Now, you know that Freud began as a somaticist, as a man who worked with the body. Then he discovered the unconscious. So he switched over into psychology. But he never forgot that he was a somaticist. *The greatest thing that ever happened in psychiatry was the discovery that the core of the neurosis was somatic, i.e., the stasis, the libido stasis was somatic.* I once treated a waiter. I did this and did that, and finally, I had to give up. I described it in *The Function*.[4] I worked an hour every day for over two years. It didn't work. Didn't work. Nothing happened, even though I went through to the urszene, to the primal scene. He had no erections, couldn't have erections. Well, such things drove me to Freud. His basic attitude about our technique was that we shouldn't be too ambitious in trying to cure. But I always had the feeling that he was very, very disappointed in the curative faculties of psychoanalysis. He had expected very much, and it didn't quite work out.[5] When I first began to analyze, treatment was to last three months, or, at the most, six months. Then it became longer and longer and longer. Then he left therapy altogether. He no longer wanted to improve humanity.

[3] Reich, here, is referring to neurasthenia as a specific example of a psychiatric disorder with a somatic core. Contrasting it with the psychoneuroses, Freud had classified neurasthenia and anxiety neuroses as actual ("aktuelle") neuroses, i.e., disturbances lacking a psychic etiology. He did go so far as to suggest that all psychoneuroses may have an actual-neurotic core, but he failed to pursue the issue. Reich, on the other hand, searching for the somatic core, found ample clinical evidence to justify the conclusion that the stasis of sexual energy was the common denominator of all neuroses. This was the starting point of his orgasm theory and all his later investigations into the nature of the sexual energy. See Documentary Supplement, p. 241. Also, Freud wrote to Reich on June 7, 1925, expressing his interest in the latter's attempts to comprehend the actual neuroses, in this instance the neurasthenia problem.

[4] *The Function of the Orgasm*, pp. 62-63.

[5] See footnote 6, p. 63.

He was disappointed, clearly disappointed. And he was right. Nothing can be done. Nothing can be done. But, to my mind, he gave up before he started. You know what I mean?

DR. EISSLER

Yes.

DR. REICH

He gave up before he started. I came to the same conclusion, but only after much experience and failure. *Nothing can be done with grown-ups.* I say this as a person who is rather experienced in psychiatry and human biology. Nothing can be done. *Once a tree has grown crooked, you can't straighten it out.* And here, just in the light of this, his rejection of the prophylaxis of the neuroses was so startling to me. If some factor makes the tree grow crooked, why don't you see how to prevent that from happening? That's quite simple. But, no, he didn't want it. Here, I lose him, as if in a fog. I think it had to do with his cancer. I can't help feeling that. He did not like people. He couldn't have any social intercourse with his students. He was cut off from social life outside. He had been very alive, and he must have suffered tremendously. Being alive, quite alive, and having to sit alone, as he sat there, is bad, very bad.

DR. EISSLER

Do you remember what he told you in discussing that waiter whom you had analyzed for two years? I'm sure it's important.

DR. REICH

He encouraged, "Gehen Sie nur vor. Deuten Sie." [6] He was really against the passive technique, but as for really concrete proposals, I'm sorry to say he didn't offer much, not much. He

6 "Just go ahead. Interpret."

couldn't concretely say, "Do that and that." There was, as yet, no theory of psychoanalytic technique.

DR. EISSLER

Your seminar was famous for that very point, that you worked out concretely the theory.[7]

DR. REICH

That's right. And, here, at this point, the theory of the therapy of the neuroses came in. Until then, nobody knew why he did what he did. Freud didn't know, either. He would say, "Be patient. Analyze. Understanding is more important than doing." Neither he, nor I, nor anybody else, at that time, knew that there is that No in the human being, that basic No, the "I won't." It is underneath the "negative therapeutic reaction." The protoplasm is just plain stuck. It cannot function properly. That is clear, now, biologically and in a practical way. That's Freud again, you see, because without his formulation of the negative therapeutic reaction and the interest that it evoked, no one could have penetrated to the answer we have today. The answer is simply that *the biological plasma function of the human race has been spoiled for millennia.*

DR. EISSLER

Did you discuss that particular subject with him—I mean the negative therapeutic reaction?

DR. REICH

Yes! Yes! Yes! I told him that I don't believe in the unconscious guilt feeling. If the "Strafbeduerfnis" [8] simply means a guilty

[7] In view of this recognition of the importance of Reich's contribution to psychoanalysis, it should be noted that in the text of Franz Alexander's *The History of Psychiatry* (1966), written in collaboration with H. G. Selznick, M.D., there is not a single reference to Reich.
[8] The need for punishment.

feeling, it's all right. In other words, if your destructiveness is just inhibited and you turn it against yourself and eat yourself up inside, then I agree with you fully. But to believe in a primary masochism, in a wish to punish yourself, in a desire to die—no! no! Freud told me explicitly, "Gehen Sie ruhig weiter mit Ihrer klinischen Arbeit. Was ich da vorgebracht habe, ist nur eine Hypothese. Sie kann stehen oder fallen. Sie ist nicht grundsatzlich wesentlich fur das Gebaude der Psychoanalyse."[9] These were approximately his words. "Gehen Sie ruhig weiter mit Ihrer klinischen Arbeit. Es war nichts mehr als ein Spiel mit Gedanken."[1] Only a hypothesis! Yet, out of that grew the horrible misuse of Thanatos.[2] I succeeded in destroying that. You know that I did?

DR. EISSLER

Yes.[3]

DR. REICH

That is dead. I think that his wish to die was somehow his own. He was sick. He was miserable. He was alone.

[9] "Just go ahead with your clinical work. What I've said here is merely hypothetical. It may, or may not, hold up. It is not basically important for the structure of psychoanalysis."
[1] "Just go ahead with your clinical work. It's nothing more than just playing with ideas."
  It is of interest to note that as late as 1937, Freud, in a letter to Princess Marie Bonaparte, advised "not to set too much value on my remarks about the destructive instinct."
[2] See excerpt from *The Function of the Orgasm*, p. 248.
[3] In *The Life and Work of Sigmund Freud*, Jones states unequivocally that there is no "primary wish for self-destruction on the part of the body; the clinical evidence points clearly in the opposite direction." It was Reich who originally opposed this concept, both theoretically and clinically. The only analysts, today, who apply the term "death instinct" in a clinical manner are, according to Jones, Melanie Klein, Karl Menninger and Hermann Nunberg.

DR. EISSLER

In what way did that cancer make itself noticeable?

DR. REICH

He couldn't speak. You see, he had been a marvelous speaker. His words flew clearly, simply, logically. I remember that Berlin Congress. He was beautiful. He spoke about "Das Ich und Das Es."[4] He spoke very clearly. And then it hit him right there in the speech organ. He had to resign. This man had wanted to talk, to go out, to speak, to move. Look at his mouth, the configuration of his mouth. He wanted to go out, to do.

DR. EISSLER

You were present when he read "Ich und Es"?

DR. REICH

Yes, yes.

DR. EISSLER

Was there a discussion?

DR. REICH

No, there was no discussion. It was very beautiful, awfully beautiful. That was the last time he spoke at a Congress. He meant something very important there, something very deep, very deep. The Ego is just as unconscious as the Id. Prächtig! Wunderbar! It takes a genius to think that way. But he never thought that the libido theory would be replaced, kicked out, with all those ego instincts.[5] Frankly, I don't understand why Karen

---

[4] *The Ego and the Id.*
[5] The so-called ego instincts are the "non-sexual" instincts. The increasing emphasis upon their importance created a dualism which made it possible to diminish the importance of the sexual instinct. According to Reich, the distinction is basically incorrect for "the ego instincts are nothing but the

Horney, Alexander, and the others did that. I don't understand. It's incredible, incredible. The libido phenomena are so obvious. Just look at any case.

By the way, I have to mention here that Horney took over my bio-energetic theory. When Freud's dualism didn't work, I proceeded toward the physiological and biological realm, and then toward the plasma motions. If I want something, I stretch out. Yes? If I am afraid, I pull in. And if I want to hit, I go out with a fury. So you have: I go out in love. I withdraw in anxiety. Or withdrawal is anxiety. That's simple. It's the plasma motion which does it. When I came to the United States, I visited Horney. She asked me about my work and I told her. Three or four years later, a book by her appeared. I don't know which it was—"Personality," or one of them. But it said she had a new theory: People are moving toward people, away from people, and against people. Toward people, away from people, against people. Do you get the point?

DR. EISSLER

Yes.

DR. REICH

But *without sex, without libido, without any bio-energy, without anything.* She did a good job in taking many things.[6]

But to come back to Freud. He was very beautiful at that

---

totality of the vegetative demands in their defense function," i.e., the ego and the id are merely different functions of the unitary biopsychic apparatus and should not be viewed as separate and distinct realms of functioning.

[6] At a conference in 1952, Reich commented on the fact that while, today, Horney and Erich Fromm are associated with the sociological application of psychoanalysis, it was actually Reich who got out and worked with the people and really began the social application of natural-scientific psychoanalysis. During those early years, Horney knew nothing of it. She and most of the other analysts were still working with individual patients.

Congress, as he always was when he spoke. Then it hit him just here, in the mouth. And that is where my interest in cancer began. I began cancer studies in 1926 or 1927.

2) OCTOBER 19, 1952

DR. EISSLER

Dr. Reich, I would like to ask about the mental-hygiene movement in which you played such a great role. I think even you originated it.

DR. REICH

No, I didn't originate the idea of the mental-hygiene movement or the fact of mental-hygiene movements. The only thing I really brought into consideration was the problem of prevention of the neuroses en masse. There was a mental-hygiene movement long before, but the recognition of the neuroses as a social problem, mass neuroses, that's what I brought into the mental-hygiene movement. Does that answer the question?

DR. EISSLER

Yes. Now, what did you do practically about it? How far did you go?

Before I did anything, I wanted to be sure that Freud was in basic agreement with me. Before incorporating the neuroses as a mass problem into mental hygiene, you first have to agree on one point, that there exists a mass neurosis, that such a thing exists at all. You see, in the psychoanalysis of the early twenties, the neurosis or the neurotic symptom was considered to be something sick in an otherwise healthy organism. That was the idea, then. It was my character analysis which introduced the basic concept that the character structure[1] is ill, sick, while the neurosis, the neurotic symptom is only an outgrowth of a general characterological condition.[2] Now, if the character neurosis is the basis of the symptom, then how widespread is it? I had made statistics in the Psychoanalytic Polyclinic, in free-thinker movements and in various associations. They revealed that about 90 percent of all women and about 70 to 80 percent of all men were just plain sick. That made me realize that there was a mass neurosis. I went to Freud. He had already said that all humanity was his patient. Here, quite concretely, was the evidence. Ninety percent of all women (today, I would say even more) are characterologically and neurotically sick and not functioning according to natural law. Now, if you exist within this realm of character-neurotic functioning,[3] then you may say

---

[1] "An individual's typical structure, his stereotyped manner of acting and reacting. The orgonomic concept of character is functional and biological and not a static, psychological or moralistic concept." *The Function of the Orgasm*, p. 359.

[2] "With character analysis it became manifest that the neurotic symptom could not possibly grow in a sound character structure, that the neurotic character was at the base of all mental distress. With these new views on human nature, the way had been opened up to question the rationality of *all* human affairs which emerged from the prevalent character structure." Reich, 1952. From the Archives of the Orgone Institute.

[3] Character neurotic: that "character which, due to chronic sexual stasis,

it is not neurotic. You may say it is "our way of life." The question is, "Is it 'our way of life,' or could it be different?" That was the point.

Now, I didn't devote myself to the mental-hygiene movement just to cure a few people or to improve their health. I started it after the fifteenth of July, 1927,[4] when a hundred people were killed and about a thousand were wounded in the street. I don't know whether you remember that?

DR. EISSLER

Yes.

DR. REICH

That gave me the jolt. Freud was on the Semmering, near Vienna, at the time, and I have a letter from him in which he asks if the world will still stand after that.[5] Shortly thereafter, I went to him and I told him I wanted to start work on a social basis. I wanted to get away from the clinics, from individual treatment, and get onto the social scene. Freud was very much for it. He saw the whole social thing. It is complete nonsense when, today, the Washington and Horney schools of psychiatry[6] say Freud refused to consider sociology. He never did. There is no trace of such a thing. I want to make that very clear. He knew exactly how things were in the world. But before he could go outside, he first had to know what was inside. He was very happy that somebody who knew the inside so well went out and tried to do

---

operates according to the principle of compulsive moral regulation." *The Function of the Orgasm*, p. 318.

[4] The reference is to the Socialist uprising in Vienna on that date.

[5] Letter from Freud to Reich, July 15, 1927.

[6] The Washington (Harry Stack Sullivan) and Horney so-called dynamic-cultural schools of psychoanalysis emphasize environmental and cultural factors in the genesis of neurosis, while tending to ignore the biological (libido).

something about it. That was what I brought into the psychoanalytic movement at that time.[7]

The first step was to establish an organization outside the psychoanalytic association. The Sozialistische Gesellschaft fuer Sexualberatung und Sexualforschung[8] was formed. I had about eight physicians and two lawyers. Among them were the Viennese psychoanalysts Annie Angel, Edmund Bergler,[9] Annie Reich. I think Sterba was also in it. In Berlin, there were Edith Jacobson, Misch, Fenichel, and many others. I spent a lot of money, thousands of shillings out of my own pocket, to get it through. I first published a notice in the Social Democratic paper, *Arbeiter Zeitung*. Then we had our first meeting, at which I spoke on neurosis as a social problem (Was it that? Or was it on sexual stauung?[1]) *You see, you couldn't get at the mental-hygiene problem with ideas such as the oedipus complex. You couldn't get at it. It didn't make sense. What made sense was the frustration, the genital frustration of the population.* Adolescents get frustrated. There is misery in marriage. Why is it so? How does it work? What can we do about it? And, here, you hit upon the social problem—the institution of marriage, laws, Catholic dogma, birth control, and all kinds of social stuff. Here we see sociology out in the open.

I discussed details with Freud and he was enthusiastic. He said, "Go ahead, just go ahead." Once a month we had a public meeting where some subject was dealt with, such as education of children or the problem of masturbation or adolescence or

[7] The story of this period in Reich's development appeared in *People in Trouble* (Orgone Institute Press, 1953).
[8] Socialist Society for Sexual Consultation and Sexual Research.
[9] Edmund Bergler, M.D., psychoanalyst; at one time assistant director of the Psychoanalytic Clinic in Vienna.
[1] Sexual stasis.

marriage or this or that. Then the people asked questions. That was quite tremendous. I still thrive on that experience. Here, the people came out completely. What I had to do, then, is very important now. What I had to do was to break through the barrier which separates the public from its own private life. You understand? Nobody talks about it. Nobody touches it. No one. No one. The first thing to do was to break through that. I told them, "I shall ask you direct questions, and I shall place before you direct issues." No circumlocution. And that worked marvelously. I shall never forget the warm, flushed faces, the glowing eyes, the tension, the contact. There's no doubt about it, Dr. Eissler, this issue will win out everywhere. It will kill any dictator. There's no doubt about the social force in it. It is the force of the future. It is the sexual revolution. What is in the way, today, is not the people, and not so much knowledge or lack of knowledge. It is Modju, the single individual, the neurotic, the pestilent character who digs here and digs there and tries to keep me from my job by keeping me busy and tying me up in legal affairs and other things.[2] I hope you get my point.

Originally, I made one mistake, one great mistake. I set it up as a political movement. Political movements were initiated because of hunger and economic needs. So I created a movement concerned with sexual needs. You see? To begin with, it was wrong to create a movement on political grounds. I know that today, but I didn't know it then. I felt that enthusiasm, that first tremendous response. That kept me going for six years. When I went up to Berlin, I lectured in mass meetings nearly— I don't know—four or five times a week. I had meetings with

---

[2] From the beginning of the attack by the Food and Drug Administration in 1947 until his imprisonment in 1957, Reich was compelled to divert much of his time and energy to legal matters.

two and three thousand people. There were meetings where Catholic priests had to answer questions on mental-hygiene problems, and so on. It was quite big. There was no organized movement in Vienna, but in Berlin there were about fifty thousand people in my organization in the first year. Any questions, please? I could go on and on, now.

DR. EISSLER
Yes. But—

DR. REICH
Yes, go ahead. Hook on to what I said.

DR. EISSLER
You touched it now, but I think there is more to say: How far you actually came to putting those plans into reality.

DR. REICH
Oh, I came very far. I came too far. I don't know whether you get me. I went too far. I would have done better if I had restricted the movement for the first ten years to the spreading of clinics. I had six clinics in Vienna where people came and received advice once or twice a week. I had one, Annie Reich had one, Annie Angel had one, Bergler had one, and so on. To provide medical and educational help was its purpose. But I went too fast. I unintentionally aroused the animosity of the political parties. They felt the power of it, and they became afraid or jealous. Their meetings were dull. They spoke about this and that, law and such things. People weren't interested. When they came to our meetings they had the whole personal, emotional life right in the open. That created too much competition. It happened too quickly, too quickly. The force of it was tremen-

dous, especially in Berlin. So, to answer your question about how far I went, I went too far.

Here, I would like to sound a warning for every future mental-hygiene movement: *Never do it the political way!* People will get very enthusiastic about it. They will glow. They will burn for you. But their structures won't follow. The character structure can't follow. Then you are in trouble. That's the danger, and that's the special problem of mental-hygiene. I'm fully occupied with it, now, in an effort to solve it. *This discrepancy between what a human being wants, what he dreams of, what he intellectually understands as true and good and what he actually can do, i.e., what his structure, the character structure, really permits him to do, is quite a problem in mental hygiene.* It is also the gap where religion comes in with the idea of paradise.[3]

So to answer your question, I went too far. It burned too much. It brought up too much enthusiasm right from the beginning. It didn't develop slowly enough. That's what killed it. And then I made enemies. Freud? I don't know. I don't think Freud was ever against it. But the psychoanalysts, socialists, communists, Nazis, yes, and the liberals—everybody was against it. All the politicians were against it. The problem is so tough, so complicated. But I did learn one thing: Never do it politically. Never do it politically. Do it factually. Establish clinics, help adolescents to establish their love lives, change the laws

---

[3] "Apart from the mass of diseases it creates, the process of armoring in early childhood makes every living expression edgy, mechanical, rigid, incapable of change and adaptation to living functions and processes. The living organ sensations, which have become inaccessible to self-perception, will, from now on, constitute the total realm of ideas which center around the 'SUPERNATURAL.' This, too, is tragically logical. Life is beyond reach, 'transcendental.' Thus, it becomes the center of religious longing for the saviour, the redeemer, the BEYOND." Reich, *Ether, God and Devil*, pp. 100-101.

which are in the way. The enthusiasm which is aroused politically does not carry you very far. It carries you far, but like a flare. Any questions? Go ahead.

DR. EISSLER

Do you remember, did Freud make any statements to you regarding his own political beliefs, where he stood politically?

DR. REICH

Politically? He always said, "I'm a scientist. I have nothing to do with politics." And since politics was hooked up with sociology, I said, "That's an impossible standpoint." You can't be apolitical in a situation such as the world was in. You know, the depression years. But he was right as far as politics went because politics is irrational. He was wrong as far as social science went. But it was not his fault because no distinction was made. We had to learn it the hard way. We had to distinguish the social from the political. He had no—yes, he had a political standpoint. It was Jewish. We spoke about it yesterday.

DR. EISSLER

But was he a Social Democrat?

DR. REICH

I don't think so.

DR. EISSLER

No?

DR. REICH

They made him a bürger of Vienna, not an ehrenbürger—they were very careful not to give too much. It was through Friedjung.[4] You know Friedjung?

[4] An early member of the Viennese psychoanalytic organization and a member of the Vienna Municipal Council.

DR. EISSLER
Yes. How was Friedjung? Did he participate in your work?

DR. REICH
Oh, yes. Friedjung cooperated with me. He gave lectures in my organization. He was a very good friend. He spoke about children. He was a good daddy and uncle. He was nice. He liked me. I liked him. Frischauf was there, too. I don't know whether you know anything about her. She was a very kind woman. She was awfully nice in her mental attitude. Do you know where they are?

DR. EISSLER
I think he was killed by the Nazis. I'm not sure.

DR. REICH
We had a Dr. Fassler who was a communist. He was killed, too. I don't know what happened to Marie Frischauf. If you hear about her, will you let me know?

DR. EISSLER
Sure, I will.

DR. REICH
Dr. Fliegl was in the movement, too. Oh, there were many. But I was careful to build up a factual, medical, educational background for the whole thing in order to be fully prepared for whatever problems might come along. Do you know what a political peddler does instead? He uses such terms as "sexual freedom," "sexual happiness for youth" as political slogans. For example, the anarchists in England, the communists in Greece do it in a political way. They promise happiness, politically. Now, that's a crime. Is that clear?

DR. EISSLER

Yes.

DR. REICH

It's a crime. *They promise happiness without really establishing the mental-hygiene requirements for it.* I never did that. I never went that way. Any questions? Go ahead.

DR. EISSLER

Yes. Did you have discussions with Freud about medicine, medical schools, and their relationship to psychoanalysis?

DR. REICH

Before I go on to that, I would like to hook on to something else I said yesterday. Freud went along with me in principle. But when it came to concrete things, such as attacking the present, compulsive family attitude, the family organization, he turned against it and he turned against me. That's very important. That's where the whole conflict started. That was what was involved at that meeting in 1929 at which I spoke of the prevention of neuroses and out of which grew his "Unbehagen in der Kultur." Mind you, he was not opposed to the basic idea. Of course, *he agreed in principle to the importance of sexual health. But he did not want what sexual health entailed, the attack on certain institutions which opposed it.* Is that clearly worked out now?

DR. EISSLER

Yes. What did Freud think of medicine, medical schools, and their relationship to psychoanalysis?

DR. REICH

Very, very little. Very, very little. He didn't like medical men at all.[5] He thought they were quacks. That's what they are. All that brain surgery,[6] all that stuff, the chemistry racket business —no good. That's medicine of the past. There's no doubt that Freud was one of the fathers of the quite new medicine—psychosomatic medicine, functional medicine. We are the pioneers in that direction. As for the old medicine, he knew what it was. He was a physician, but he was not a member of any A.M.A., you understand. Do you know the difference? He was a very good physician, but he was not enthusiastic about the methods of medicine or the chauvinism of any medical association, especially as it has developed here in the U.S.A. But I want you to understand that it has to be that way with the A.M.A.'s. There's so much cheating in the field of medicine, especially in the United States, cheating, cheats, just quacks, that I understand why they become chauvinistic and bureaucratic. That's only a remark about the logic in the irrational. No, he didn't think very highly of official medicine. However, he defended the quack in psychiatry. He made grave mistakes there. I think it was a very great mistake in his fight against the chauvinism in medicine when he protected Reik. Theodor Reik was in trouble once in Vienna. He was attacked by someone for practicing medicine. Freud supported him. And from that, "lay analysis" developed. Freud gave very strong support to the lay analyst.[7] I don't know how you feel about it, but I tell you quite frankly I think Freud

[5] "To medicine itself he felt no direct attraction. He did not conceal in later years that he never felt at home in the medical profession, and that he did not seem to himself to be a regular member of it." Ernest Jones, *The Life and Work of Sigmund Freud,* Vol. I, p. 27.
[6] Reich is referring to the frontal lobotomy which gained some vogue in the treatment of mental disease.
[7] Among the early lay analysts were the Reverend Oskar Pfister, Otto Rank, Siegfried Bernfeld, Theodor Reik, Anna Freud, Ernst Kris and Robert Wälder.

made a very grave mistake. The admission of lay analysts into natural scientific psychoanalysis was a very great mistake. Here, again, I refer to the natural scientific angle in psychoanalysis as opposed to the mere psychological angle. The psychological angle doesn't carry you anywhere. You have to be rooted in natural scientific thinking, in physical medicine, and so on. You have all these lay analysts in the United States and, in my opinion, they do very much damage, very great damage. And it was Freud who opened the way to that. That's what I can't help feeling.[8]

DR. EISSLER

Did you also discuss with Freud those movements which came out of analysis, like Adler and Jung? [9]

DR. REICH

Oh, yes. Oh, yes. There was never disagreement on such things. It was quite clear where Adler[1] was wrong. He got stuck in a very superficial layer with the power thing and he didn't think further. It was an evasion of the libido theory. That was quite clear. Freud was very clear about these things. He had an awfully clear mind. He knew. He had his logic in his hands. He

[8] "Foreseeing that the topic [lay analysis] was going to be one of major interest at the next Congress, to be held in Innsbruck in September, 1927, Eitingon and I arranged for a preliminary discussion in the form of contributions to be published in the *International Journal* and the *Zeitschrift*, the official organs of the Association. Twenty-eight such contributions, including two final ones by Freud and Eitingon respectively, were published in the form of a literary symposium." Jones, *The Life and Work of Sigmund Freud*, Vol. III, p. 293.
    Reich contributed to this symposium. See excerpt from his article, p. 251.
[9] See Documentary Supplement, p. 261.
[1] Alfred Adler, M.D. (1870-1937)—Austrian psychiatrist, founder of the school of individual psychology and proponent of the concept of the will to power as the central issue in the neurotic process, denoting the compensatory strivings against feelings of inadequacy and inferiority.

knew he was a bit wrong with Adler, too. I have a letter to Ferenczi where I complained that Freud wronged Adler at one spot.[2] You see, Adler really went into the ego psychology, but he did it the wrong way. That didn't mean that he was basically wrong. Freud attacked him from the standpoint of the libido theory. He rebuffed him and didn't want anything of the ego theory. Then, Freud himself went into it, undermining the libido theory. Still, such conflicts are bound to happen in a scientific movement. But Adler was a run-away.

DR. EISSLER

And Jung?[3]

DR. REICH

Jung? No, I don't remember any special discussions about that conflict. Oh, yes! Oh, yes! There was one thing, and Freud was wrong there, too. Jung meant something very important. You know what he meant? He really meant the energy in the universe,[4] a universal libido. Freud said it was not scientific.[5] You couldn't measure it on a Geiger counter as I can.[6] Furthermore, it was mystically conceived. So Freud was correct in rejecting it

2 See letter, p. 145.
3 Carl Gustav Jung, M.D. (1875-1961)—Swiss psychoanalyst, founder of a school of analytic psychology utilizing, in addition to the personal unconscious arising during the individual's finite existence, the concept of the "collective unconscious," a repository of "mystical, collective ideas" arising from the "inherited possibility of psychic functioning in general."
4 Reference to Jung's "universal unconscious."
5 "All that has been gained from psychoanalytic observation thus far is relinquished if one follows the procedure of C. G. Jung in subtilizing the concept of the libido, permitting it to coincide with psychic instinctive energy in its totality." Sigmund Freud, *Three Contributions to the Theory of Sex*, p. 76.
6 The Geiger-Müller counter is used to measure orgone energy in the atmosphere.

in that form. He also didn't like the anti-Semitism which came into it? [7]

Oh, yes. Now I remember where Jung came into debates. I tended, then, toward a unification of the instinct theory. That means that all the many instincts we have—oral, anal, and so on—would have some common root, whereas, in Freud, they stand out as single pillars. I was already on the way to that unification of the partial instincts in a common biological principle. But I had to guard against Jung because he had mystified the whole thing. Freud held on to his dualism. He said there must be two separate, opposing forces. Two forces. That was in connection with a discussion of the death instinct. When I asked him whether masochism was primary or secondary, whether it is a turned-back sadism or aggression or a disturbance of aggression outward, or whether it's a primary death instinct thing, Freud, peculiarly, maintained both. He said that, clinically, masochism is secondary, but, in the basic theoretical sense, there must be a death instinct. And wrong as Freud was with the death instinct, wrong as he was, he was right even there. What he felt with the death instinct, what he tried to catch there, what he felt in the human being was a certain dying quality. We call it DOR today in a physical sense.[8] There is a deadly orgone energy. It is in the atmosphere. You can demonstrate it on devices such as the Geiger counter. It's a swampy quality. You know what swamps are? Stagnant, deadly water which doesn't flow, doesn't metabolize. Cancer, too, is due to a stagnation. *Cancer is due to a stagnation*

[7] "Jung had generalized the concept of libido to such an extent as to make it completely lose its meaning of sexual energy. He ended up with the 'collective unconscious' and with that, in mysticism, which he later, as a national socialist, officially represented." *The Function of the Orgasm*, p. 127.

[8] Deadly orgone energy: stagnant, decaying energy in the living organism and in the atmosphere.

of the flow of the life energy in the organism. So Freud was trying to grasp that quality. I know, today, that *he sensed something in the human organism which was deadly.*[9] *But he thought in terms of instinct. So he hit upon the term "death instinct." That was wrong. "Death" was right. "Instinct" was wrong. Because it's not something the organism wants. It's something that happens to the organism. Therefore, it is not an "instinct."* Freud was very deep in that. He had a nose for such things Tremendous! Tremendous! Tremendous! He was theoretically very good. You must grant mistakes to a man who has to handle such a vast realm as the unconscious. Everybody makes mistakes.

DR. EISSLER
Did he say, did he tell you something about Stekel? [1]

DR. REICH
I don't know whether we ever talked about Stekel. One thing is clear: I know that he didn't like it if we, as students, associated with people whom he had discarded. Yes. He thought Stekel was a charlatan.[2] I think he was unjust to Stekel. Stekel did things. He slept with patients and such things. Freud didn't like

---

9 "The moment a man questions the meaning and value of life, he is sick, since objectively neither has any existence; by asking this question one is merely admitting to a store of unsatisfied libido to which something else must have happened, a kind of fermentation leading to sadness and depression." Sigmund Freud, in a letter to Princess Marie Bonaparte, August 13, 1937. From *Letters of Sigmund Freud*, selected and edited by Ernst L. Freud (New York: McGraw-Hill, 1964), p. 436.
1 Wilhelm Stekel (1868-1940), German psychoanalyst, proponent of an active intervention technique to shorten the duration of treatment, relying to a considerable extent on his own intuition.
2 Regarding Stekel, Freud is quoted as having said, "He plays the respectful disciple, and meantime assumes the privilege of a superior. He forgives me so to speak for all that he has done to me." Joseph Wortis, *Fragment of an Analysis with Freud* (New York: Simon and Schuster, 1954).

that. I think that was his reason. I'm not too sure. Stekel was superficial, very superficial. He was too quick. He tried to get at the answers too quickly. He had answers to all things, right away.

DR. EISSLER

And Rank?[3]

DR. REICH

He liked Rank very much.

DR. EISSLER

There was no disagreement yet, at that time?

DR. REICH

No, not at that early time. It began about 1923 or 1924. I remember that Freud was very decent in this conflict with Rank, but Rank was very wrong. Again, Rank hit upon something very true. Rank said something very real, without knowing it. It is what we operate with today in our children's clinic. It is the tight uterus, the contracted, spastic uterus which chokes the child. The oxygen is lacking. The CO_2 is excessive. Then, coming out of such a spastic uterus is really a trauma. The birth process takes twenty to forty hours in primaparae as against one to five hours in relaxed organisms. So Rank was in the right direction, too. But what did he do? Just as so many others did, just as Adler did with the will to power. They based everything on it. They made a secondary or tertiary process the sole, responsible factor. And Rank did the same thing.[4] That is no good. *It is not*

---

[3] Otto Rank (1884-1939), Viennese psychoanalyst who maintained that the act of being born is a shock or trauma, thus of great consequence in the development of the psyche. Freud felt that Rank overestimated its influence.

[4] "Rank also was aware of the inadequacies of technique. He recognized the longing for peace, for return to the womb. He misunderstood the fear

good science to take a secondary principle and attach primary importance to it.

Freud, on the other hand, was mainly a dialectician, a functionally thinking human being. He always wanted two forces to counteract each other. What he did not do, and I don't know why, was to see that *these two opposite forces were actually one in the depth because everything opposed in nature is ultimately a unit.* Yes, a unit. Do I make myself clear? Of course they split up. Did you see our sign on the observatory? It's over the door. Look at it when you walk out. Are you familiar with the sign? [5] *Out of a unitary force a splitting, an antithesis develops.* That is my way of thinking about natural scientific things. Now, Freud had these rigid ideas about instincts. He was a bit rigid there. But he was always separating his speculations from his theories. That was why he always said, "Gehen Sie nur ruhig weiter Ihren Weg. Machen Sie Ihre Klinik. Es spielt keine Rolle, primarer Masochismus oder Todestrieb." [6] It did later. You know what the psychoanalysts did with so many different things.[7] Here, I am a bit emotional because I had such a hard time combating this with my character analysis. Any questions?

---

of living in this terrible world and misinterpreted it in a biological sense as the trauma of birth, which he supposed to be the nucleus of the neurosis. He failed to ask himself why people longed to get away from real life and back into the protective womb. He came into conflict with Freud, who continued to adhere to the libido theory, and became an outsider." *The Function of the Orgasm*, p. 127.

[5] Reich refers to the symbol of the common functioning principle signifying a unitary principle from which two antithetical principles are derived, making them identical and antithetical at the same time.

[6] "Just go your own way. Do your clinical work. Primary masochism or the death instinct plays no role."

[7] The overvaluation of Freud's speculations.

DR. EISSLER

If I may switch to an entirely different topic—

DR. REICH

Yes, go ahead.

DR. EISSLER

What about discussions regarding religion and church, and so on? Do you remember that that played quite a role?

DR. REICH

I don't remember ever having discussed problems of religion and church. I encountered enough of it outside, of course. I may have discussed it with Freud. I don't know. Perhaps it appeared in a different form. Freud was an intellectual individual. He believed in the overpowering role of the mind, i.e., of the intellect as against emotions. You know his basic attitude toward emotions. Not that emotions are bad, but you have to get them out of the way. You have to control everything. Your intellect and mind must be master of the emotions. But that attitude came into conflict with the direction which the work in genitality took, where the emotions are involved, the "streaming," the feeling in the body. Freud rejected the existence of so-called "ozeanische Gefühle." [8] He didn't believe in such a thing. I never quite understood why. It is so obvious that the "ozeanische Gefühle," the feeling of unity between you and Spring and God, or what people call God, and Nature is a very basic element in all religion, in all religious feeling to the extent that it is not sick and distorted. Freud rejected that. And I regret to say, I had the feeling that *in the process of subduing his*

[8] Oceanic feelings.

own *aliveness, his own biological aliveness, he had to restrict himself, to sublimate, to live in a way he didn't like, and to resign.* I had the feeling that he, somehow, couldn't accept the concept which is behind all good religion. Do you get my point? All good religion. I am referring to the biological activity in your organism which is a part of the universe. He rejected it. And I know he didn't like it. He didn't like it. Now, my work developed in just that direction. In the schizophrenic, for example, the streaming they feel, the emotions they feel, that's all very real. And, somehow, Freud couldn't follow that. His work became intellectualized. And, to my mind, that was a part of the bad development that took place. He was caught in words. He was caught in words.

DR. EISSLER

Dr. Reich, you wanted to make a statement about Federn. Do you remember? A document regarding Federn?

DR. REICH

Oh, I shall write one out about Federn. There's something I have to say. I don't want to say it here. I shall write it out and send you the document. I would like to have it deposited. It has something to do with me privately, something very private about myself. I may deposit it in a sealed envelope. It must be on record. So in case something turns up, this envelope may be opened. Do you understand?

DR. EISSLER

Yes.

DR. REICH

Should some defamation or slander come up any time, then this would answer it.

DR. EISSLER

Yes, certainly.

DR. REICH

Did the "ozeanische Gefühle" problem settle the religious question?

DR. EISSLER

Yes.

DR. REICH

It did in a broad sense. Freud was an agnostic. He was a Freidenker. But that doesn't solve the problem of religion or of religious feeling in people. Don't you think we should conclude shortly?

DR. EISSLER

Yes.

DR. REICH

Do you have any other questions?

DR. EISSLER

You perhaps remember still some personal anecdotes or personal experiences?

DR. REICH

You mean about Freud?

DR. EISSLER

Little things, yes, habits he had—

DR. REICH

Well, I never paid too much attention to these things. I know that he didn't like it when Rie's daughter cut her hair short. She came home with a Bubikopf. He disliked it intensely. That's gossip. Shall we go into that?

DR. EISSLER

I think gossip—for the historian, gossip is extremely important.

DR. REICH

Do I have to take part in that? Well, there was a question whether Anna Freud had a love life. That was a very much discussed thing. Many analysts in Vienna thought she lived in abstinence. And it was regretted. I, personally, felt somehow that it wasn't good for the development of the education of children. Problems of genitality arise in education and if one of its leaders lives that way it is important. This is what everybody felt. I know nothing about her. I wouldn't like to utter any opinions about it. Is that clear enough?

DR. EISSLER

Yes.

DR. REICH

Other anecdotes? I don't know. Once, as a young physician, he came home drunk at night, or something of that kind, was brought home drunk. Such things— But he did not discuss that. Oh, yes. He used to analyze his children. If the child had wet himself, he would ask, "Why did you do it?"

He was not sarcastic, but he used a biting wit to whip people. Snap! He was very sharp. He never did it with me. Never! With me, he was oh, mad, mad, later—in the late thirties.[9] —Oh, Silberer. You know that Silberer committed suicide?

[9] In 1952, when Reich was rereading Freud's letters to him, he commented that, for the first time, he felt a certain fear on the part of Freud toward him.

DR. EISSLER

Yes.

DR. REICH

After meeting Freud. Tausk,[1] I think, went this way, too. Freud liked Helene Deutsch very much.

DR. EISSLER

Yes?

DR. REICH

He liked pretty women. For instance, Princess Bonaparte[2] was quite pretty at that time, and Deutsch was a very pretty woman. Want more of such gossip?

DR. EISSLER

Sure.

DR. REICH

You know who knew the gossip. Psychoanalytic "Tratsch" was a foible with Fenichel. He wrote letters around about what everybody did to everybody else. Do you know that?

DR. EISSLER

I didn't know that.

DR. REICH

He did. Oh, yes! You would like to have them?

DR. EISSLER

Yes.

DR. REICH

Then you can read about all kinds of things psychoanalysts did.

[1] Victor Tausk (1877-1919), author of a work on schizophrenia.
[2] Princess Marie Bonaparte (1882-1962), personal friend of Freud who, in 1926, founded the Société Psychanalytique de Paris.

I wouldn't like to go into it. I didn't like it. Later, I became a victim of that gossip. I have them in a heap. That was long ago, eighteen years ago.

DR. EISSLER

Yes, that, I think, may be an important historical document in a hundred years.

DR. REICH

You would like this? Tell me, how far do you go when you mean Freud, when you say Freud, Sigmund Freud Archives? How far do you go?

DR. EISSLER

Well, it's difficult to say. It originally meant Freud, and just Freud, but I don't think that you can really make sharp distinctions.

DR. REICH

Yes, that's right. There's no limitation because he influenced so much. But, to me, it's quite a dead period—this whole thing. It is meaningful from a point of view of my own use, of my early development, my emotional connection with Freud. I liked him very much. He liked me very much. It was important. But it is only a memory now. The psychoanalysts still think I'm a psychoanalyst. No! No! Am I looked upon as a psychoanalyst?

DR. EISSLER

It's difficult to say. I mean, your historical role certainly was that of an analyst.

DR. REICH

Oh, yes. But I have had nothing to do with it for twenty years. I wouldn't like to be called a psychoanalyst. Not because I despise the psychoanalyst. No. It's a very great thing. But because I have nothing to do with it.[3]

Are you satisfied with the interview?

DR. EISSLER

Yes. I am certainly very grateful.

DR. REICH

I hope it will—

DR. EISSLER

And I could imagine that when you read the transcript that many more things may come to your mind.

DR. REICH

Yes, that's possible. I am very careful in historical matters, with good reason. I think it will take hundreds of years before the theory of the unconscious and the theory of bio-energy will be really lived by alive people. And to protect that process, you have to guard against slander. Slander will go on for a long time —the slander of love, the slander of genitality, the slander of life, the hate of life—for a long time. To protect against that is part of the job. It is beyond psychoanalysis. It has nothing to do with psychoanalysis. It is outside.

[3] "Your suggestion to link up the discovery of the Life Energy with Freud's contributions to science cannot be put into effect. There is no such link. The utmost station of my work process which had clear cut positive links with psychoanalysis is the presentation in the *second* edition of my *Character Analysis*. Even these positive links had been rejected by Freud, including the crucial orgasm theory, the starting point of the later orgone energy developments." Reich, in a letter to Dr. Harry Slochower, January 3, 1956.

3) OCTOBER 19, 1952

(continued)

DR. REICH

Now, you asked me to tell you about the private affairs of the psychoanalysts. Not because we are interested in private affairs as such—we are, of course, as physicians, as scientists—but because they had, as I said, some influence on the development of psychoanalysis. It is a very tough chapter, a very unpleasant one, but I think it is necessary.[1] I hope to do it with the least possible harm.

I may introduce it with the following words: You see, the great man, the pioneer, the one who invented something, or did something, is in the public spotlight. Everybody looks at him; everybody criticizes him; everybody wants to know how many

[1] "What is at stake at this point are the personal *backstage events and emotional involvements* of those who helped to build up psychiatry in the early part of this century. These emotional involvements are socially of such a crucial nature that perfect clarity is required on the part of all participants regarding the *dynamic* structure of the undertaking." Reich, 1952. From the Archives of the Orgone Institute.

women he had; whether he was divorced or not divorced; how many times he was divorced, and so on and so on. But those who ask these questions and those who assume the right to delve into the private lives of the pioneer, mostly to do damage, are themselves hidden in the bushes. I have a very typical picture of that. The pioneer is like a deer in the open meadow, and all of his critics and all of his enemies are all around him in the bushes. They can shoot from ambush and he can't do a thing about it. Now, Freud was a pioneer, and you know how people wanted to know about him. He ran away from that. I told you that yesterday. He stayed at home. He didn't see people. He was careful about his private life. He went into the sublimation theory.

Now, I myself began to be a pioneer, about 1923, when I discovered the genitality problem in neurosis. And the enemies —they were not enemies yet, but they sensed danger. As I told you yesterday, most of the psychoanalysts had been patients, sexually disturbed themselves, and that had a great influence. But it wouldn't have developed as it did if I hadn't tackled the problem of genitality in the neuroses. So the spotlight was turned on to me very early. I remember, in this connection, a remark by Reik, Theodor Reik, when I gave my first lecture on "die Rolle der Gentalität in der Neurosenetiologie." [2] All of the Viennese psychoanalysts sat there and listened. They were very attentive. Then, for the first time, the emotional atmosphere around me cooled. Reik said that it was a perfect presentation, but "I wouldn't like to have written that book." That was his remark. I think that characterizes the whole situation.

About 1926, when I published the work on the genitality in children, the first puberty, rumors came to my ears that I cohab-

[2] The role of genitality in the etiology of the neuroses.

ited with my patients. I didn't. It was Federn who slandered. That went on and on and on, underhandedly. I would hear something here, something there.

To further illustrate the situation as it developed around 1932 —I was in trouble with my wife, my first wife. You know that?

DR. EISSLER

Yes.

DR. REICH

She was sick. I just had to leave her. And I, in contradistinction to Freud, did not give up my private life. I lived my love life. I was not afraid of public opinion. When the relationship with my first wife did not work out, I took another woman. Today, such things are readily acknowledged, aren't they? But in those "cultured" Viennese circles it was something very peculiar. Now, I was in the open. Everybody knew about it. I was not promiscuous, or in any way amoral or immoral. But I never permitted my organism to grow stale or to become dirty. That goes very deep, you understand. You know what happens when somebody lives too long in abstinence. He gets dirty, dirty-minded, pornographic, neurotic, and so on. I never permitted that to happen to me. *One only shrinks if one lives against nature.* One shrinks, gets sick, ill, in one way or another. I never permitted that to happen. My life was an open secret, or, I should say, quite in the open. On the other hand, the private lives of the analysts were very much hidden. However, through analysis, and so on, we knew what was going on. As a psychoanalyst, you are aware of the fact that the one who leads a frustrated life, or a pathological life, is envious of the one who doesn't, the one who leads a clear and straight life. I never made any bones about it. I didn't talk about it. I didn't carry it ahead of me. But I didn't hide it. I didn't have anything to hide. When I was through with my first wife, I had a second one. I wasn't married to her, not legally married to her, but she was my wife. That was Elsa Lindenberg. So you see, while I was in the open with my genital relationships to women, they were hidden. I don't think it is right that I should divulge names, but I can assure you that many things went on in a clandestine manner and, sometimes, in a dirty manner. Without mentioning names, I shall mention facts which resulted from the genital frustration of some psychoanalysts. Do you follow me clearly?

DR. EISSLER

Yes.

DR. REICH

There were instances where psychoanalysts, under the pretext of a genital examination, of a medical examination, put their fingers into the vaginas of their patients. It was quite frequent. I knew that. You see, it happened once or twice that I fell in love with a patient. Then I was frank about it. I stopped the treatment and I let the thing cool off. Then we decided either yes or no to go to bed. Is that clear?

DR. EISSLER

Yes.

DR. REICH

I was quite straight about it. Some psychoanalysts didn't do that. They would be hypocrites about it. They would pretend there was nothing there and would masturbate the patient during the sessions.

DR. EISSLER

Yes.

Now, that not only created very bad situations, but it also created a bad conscience or an envy toward me who was different in these matters. It is quite clear that the man who discovered the genitality function in neurosis and elaborated the orgastic potency question could not himself live in a sick way. A sick organism could not have found the way to these problems, anyway. So there was envy there. There was envy on the part of the restricted one toward the one who didn't permit himself to be restricted.

One way the world usually attempts to kill the pioneer is to segregate him, to put him away into loneliness, into lonesomeness, so he can't live a normal life. That is one way of breaking him. It happened to Nietzsche, for example. Now, I never permitted anyone to do that to me. They tried many times.[3] What did I do? I dissolved the organizations that tried to do that. Do you follow my point?

DR. EISSLER

No—the last one I don't.

DR. REICH

You don't. Well, for example, it happened recently in New York. There was a group of two dozen or so physicians who began to admire me and to have this mystical attitude toward me. They sat around me. They made that bust of me[4] and carried it up and down the steps in my house and made a holy smoke out of me. That began to disturb my life, my vitality. I

[3] The jailing of Reich achieved for his enemies what he had been able to avoid during so much of his eventful life. It was the final and tragically irrevocable solution to the endless attempts to segregate him. Jailing succeeded where slander and defamation had failed.

[4] Reich refers to the bust of him by Jo Jenks, 1949. It is now on his tomb at Orgonon. See photograph, following p. 142.

had to separate myself. I didn't want it. It is much more important that I stay alive and do my experiments and my science than it is to have a few followers. This is only to show you the way I was. I was that way all the while, all through. But the others were different. I don't say they are dirty, but they are hypocrites, just plain hypocrites. For instance, I was reproached because I married a former patient of mine, Annie Pink.[5] It turned out very badly. Rado married a patient, Emmy. Others married patients. There was nothing wrong with that. What was wrong, however, was the hypocrisy which was in many treatments—directly there—on the spot. And that created a bad conscience. And a bad conscience creates, as you well know, malignant behavior. *You make somebody else bad in order to free yourself from responsibility. We call that the Emotional Plague.* In brief, I am aware of the fact that Jones and Federn tried to present me to Freud as an immoral individual. I am quite sure about Federn, not so sure about Jones.

There is something wrong when most psychiatrists and analysts regard normal, natural genitality as psychopathic, or when they confuse a healthy genital character with a schizophrenic simply because both are quite different from the average, armored, neurotic human being. I don't want to go into that now. It is too complicated. I only want to say that the analysts used underhanded means to turn Freud against me—Freud, who was on best terms with me, who expected very much from me. I am sure that documents will turn up to that effect. If I am wrong, then I am sorry. Then I misjudged the whole situation, you understand. I don't think I am wrong. If it is not contained in documents, then it was expressed in mere hearsay and gossip.

[5] Reich's first wife, Annie Reich Rubinstein, M.D. See Documentary Supplement, pp. 225, 232, 236.

This was not a special case of hate, or infamy, or destructiveness toward me. It is a general thing that goes on everywhere. But the psychoanalysts are no different from anyone else. They are not exempt from it. I mention it to give you an example of *the sexual situation among psychoanalysts* which, of course, *was decisive with regard to their obscuring the sexual etiology of the neurosis*. Do I make myself clear?

DR. EISSLER

Yes.

DR. REICH

If the analysts were disturbed to such an extent, then the main accomplishment of Freud, namely, the discovery of the sexual etiology of the neurosis, couldn't survive. I assure you that it is the same with the orgonomists today with the genitality theory. They don't touch it. These *armored character structures cannot handle natural genitality*. It may take another fifty years or so to get it across.

Let me give you another example. My second wife, Elsa Lindenberg, was very beautiful. That is her picture over there. I came to the Lucerne Congress with her in 1934. It is quite amusing to think back on that today. But to give you a picture of the attitude of some analysts at that time: They lived in hotels, sat around in smoky lobbies, and so on. I didn't. I lived with my wife in a tent at the Lucerne Lake. I had a dagger, you know, as you have when camping. Today, nobody would find anything peculiar in it. Fifteen years later, a rumor went around in New York to the effect that I had gone completely crazy at Lucerne and had put up a tent in the lobby of the hotel and that I went around with a dagger. You never knew who started it, but that rumor went around and came back to me. It was true that I lived in a tent, but not in the lobby. And it was true I had a dagger, but not at the convention. You know how that is "verdictet" [condensed]. When my wife appeared there, many analysts just streamed at her, as males do, trying to get to her. Only sex-hungry, starved individuals do that. Is that clear?

DR. EISSLER

Yes.

DR. REICH

Only starved, genitally starved individuals do such things. A genital character, a normal, healthy individual doesn't do that. It doesn't occur to him to do such things, to run after a woman in such a manner. They didn't know that she was my wife, but when they found out, they retreated. To get to the essence of the whole thing, it is impossible for a human organism, such as that of an analyst, to work continuously over the years with the human structure, with the instincts, the perverted instincts and the healthy instincts, to take all that, to have to accept it, to have it poured onto him, and to stand it, unless he himself is completely clean, lucid, and orgastically satisfied, unless he himself lives in a good way. Now, that was not the case with the majority of psychoanalysts. And that is crucial. Here is the structure, the character structure, that had its hand in destroying the basic Freudian theory, the sexual etiology of the neurosis. That was the basic thing it did. They got away from natural genitality. And why did they get away from it? They couldn't stand it. Their structures couldn't stand it. I don't think they avoided it in a moral way. In some cases, they did so in a pornographic way; in others, in a defensive, compulsion neurotic way; in still others, by just not having contact with it, just not handling it. I had many cases from psychoanalysts, and it is true that they

107)   *The Interview*

don't handle the genital problem of a patient. That is quite generally true. I knew it as early as 1926, 1927. I spoke to Freud about it. But, at that time, I didn't know the extent of the hatred against the normal, against the natural. So you follow me?

DR. EISSLER

Yes.

DR. REICH

The hatred against the natural, the sick against the healthy, is the major realm of my psychiatric endeavor today. I call the problem the *Emotional Plague,* and I see it in a biological way. But, at that time, I didn't know all of that. It only became clear much later. Still, I was always astonished: "*Why, in heaven's name, do you persecute the normal, the natural?*" I remember that discussions on this subject were rather frequent. And Freud had nothing to say. He didn't understand it, either. I, somehow, had the feeling that he didn't want to touch it. He didn't want to touch it. I don't know whether you want to go into that. It is a very important point. That was not Freud's personal thing—not that he was a coward, not that he was sick himself. I don't think so. I think he was quite a lively structure. It has to do with something much bigger than that. I don't know whether you want to go into it.

DR. EISSLER

Yes.

DR. REICH

Sure? It goes very deep. I don't know whether you are acquainted with the orgonomic picture of the structure of the human character—the "core," the "middle layer," and the "periphery." It gives one a very practical tool with which to work with patients. It is a bio-energetic tool. You can't get at the human character by psychoanalytic means. You have to reach it with character analysis or orgone therapy. Human beings live emotionally on the surface, with their surface appearance. Correct? In order to get to the core where the natural, the normal, the healthy is, you have to get through that middle layer. And in that middle layer there is terror. There is severe terror. Not only that, there is murder there. All that Freud tried to subsume under the death instinct is in that middle layer. He thought it was biological. It wasn't. It is an artifact of culture. It is a structural malignancy of the human animal. Therefore, before you can get through to what Freud called Eros or what I call orgonotic streaming or plasmatic excitation (the basic plasma action of the bio-energetic system), you have to go through hell. Just through hell! This is true for the physician as well as the patient. In this hell, there is confusion, schizophrenic breakdown, melancholic depression. They are all there. I have this in *Character Analysis*. I don't have to repeat it. But why bring the Life Force in here? There is only one reason: To show you why nobody wanted to touch it or to get at the biological core where I was working at that time. Before you can reach that core, you must encounter hate, terror, murder. All these wars, all the chaos now —do you know what that is to my mind? *Humanity is trying to get at its core, at its living, healthy core. But before it can be reached, humanity has to pass through this phase of murder, killing and destruction.* What Freud called the destructive instinct is in the middle layer. A bull is mad and destructive when it is frustrated. Humanity is that way, too. That means that before you can get to the real thing—to love, to life, to rationality —you must pass through hell. This has very grave implications for social development. I don't want to go into it now, but

I wanted to explain why the psychoanalysts refused, unconsciously, to touch what I was working with. If I had fully known its consequences, I would have run myself. I don't want to make myself better than the others, you understand. At that time, I would have run. I couldn't run today. The bridges are burned behind me. Looking back, I understand it. It is very dangerous. You see, the armor, as thick as it is and as bad as it is, is a protective device, and it is good for the individual under present social and psychological circumstances to have it. He couldn't live otherwise. That is what I try to teach my doctors today. I tell them I am glad they don't succeed in breaking down that armor because people, who have grown up with such structures, are used to living with them. If you take that away, they break down. They can't, they just can't live any longer. They can't function, you see. It will take a long time—maybe decades, maybe centuries, I don't know—until we have new generations whose structures will be different. But there is no doubt, if you would break down all of the armoring in the world today, there would be chaos. Perfect chaos! Murder everywhere! There is a rational element here. And the reason why I was in trouble with the analysts was that there was not only the structural but also this rational element. So I knew where the dangers were. But the analysts refused to even look at it. Do you get me now? They refused to even look at it. Their structures did not permit them to really understand the rational. It was their frustrated structures that blocked access to the whole problem. They could not reach it because of their hatred of the natural. *To this day, genitality doesn't exist in psychoanalysis.* You know that. I will tell you more. *It doesn't exist anywhere, not even in my own organization.* You just can't tackle it. Now, that was the background of the situation, the real background. But I didn't know it then.

Nobody knew it. It only came out later. I lived what I would call a determinedly healthy, genital, love life. I didn't permit anyone to frustrate my emotional health. The analysts didn't grasp that. Is that clear? I wasn't promiscuous. I did not do immoral things. In general, it was always clean and clear. I always had my woman. They didn't. They lived in marriages they hated. I broke up my marriage when it threatened to destroy my work. When I couldn't stand it any more, I left. And that seemed impossible to them. Now, that is the background of the defamation. Does that cover it now? Do you have any questions?

DR. EISSLER

I understand that you don't want to go into details.

DR. REICH

Oh yes, I want to go into details, but only into pertinent details.

DR. EISSLER

You mentioned yesterday about Jones. I thought that that had a direct effect on—

DR. REICH

Oh yes, of course. He was a very frustrated Englishman, you see. And he hated the way I lived. So, to judge from the events at Lucerne, he most likely dug against me to Freud. He thought I was psychopathic. The analysts don't distinguish the sick and the healthy. So, to them, I was psychopathic.

DR. EISSLER

And Rado—what was Rado's part?

DR. REICH

Oh, that—I am not sure about depositing that, but I will tell you the story. It was this: Emmy, his wife, and I had very strong genital contact with each other. Never anything like full embrace happened between us, but we danced a lot together and we had very strong contact. And Rado was jealous.

DR. EISSLER

And then he started an intrigue against you?

DR. REICH

Yes. He was the one who started that rumor in 1934. He began the rumor that I was schizophrenic. He was the one. And Fenichel picked it up. The rumor was that I was in a mental institution. I wasn't. I never was, never have been. Fenichel was the one who broke down emotionally. It was Fenichel who was in an institution for three weeks after a breakdown. He broke down in connection with my separation from the IPA. I never mentioned him by name, but I related that whole story in *Character Analysis,* in the third edition.[6] I never reacted to that publicly because I knew I was strong enough to survive. So, to begin with, it was Rado because of Emmy. Fenichel and others picked it up easily, as usually happens. I had quite a time to get rid of that. The rumor preceded me by a year in the United States. Everybody thought I was psychotic. That was my punishment for the discovery of the orgasm function.

As I mentioned before, the analysts don't touch it.

This "don't touch it" showed up quite clearly in the handling of the Freud Archives. I don't know whether you know that. Freud was put away: Nobody wants to deal with Freudian problems, you understand. "Put them away for a hundred years. Let two or three later generations decide about it. We don't want anything of it." You won't agree with me. There is, however, no

6 See excerpt from *Character Analysis,* p. 230.

doubt about it. When your secretary went down to the Library of Congress to confirm receipt of my documents, the answer I received back was the assurance that my correspondence with Freud or about Freud is put away for a hundred years. But I am not interested in that. I never intended to put away my correspondence for a hundred years. On the contrary, I am going to publish it during my lifetime.[7] There is nothing to hide. Are you going to tell them what I say? [8]

DR. EISSLER

Yes.

DR. REICH

Everyone wants to try to put Freud and the whole subject away. They don't want to touch it really, fully. They don't want to handle it. They want nothing of it.[9] That's a basic human characteristic that acts everywhere in psychiatry. The puberty problem, the adolescent problem—nobody touches it. You see the connection? Freud himself put away a lot of his own true being and discoveries. The pressure of the emotional plague is too great and dangerous to carry.

DR. EISSLER

Yes.

DR. REICH

I have that point off my chest now.

When I worked in the socialist and the communist groups in

---

[7] See Documentary Supplement, Correspondence, p. 138ff.
[8] "It is not simply a question of depositing a few documents with the Library of Congress, sealed off against inspection for 100 years . . . it is a *present-day* general and crucial problem of 'social psychiatry.'" Reich, 1952. From the Archives of the Orgone Institute.
[9] *Sigmund the Unserene—A Tragedy in Three Acts* by Percival Bailey is a clear expression of the prevalent trend to discredit Freud and dispose of him.

Vienna from 1927 to 1930, the analysts said that I was a communist.[1] It was a handy tool for my enemies, you know. I wasn't a communist. I wasn't a Marxist. I understood Marx, but I saw that Marxism, as I proved in my writings, was insufficient to handle the problems. But the analysts were already afraid of the "social consequences." If I had known where it would lead, I would have been afraid, too. But I didn't, you see. I was determined to go right after the problem. There was the marriage situation. Infantile genitality. The puberty, the adolescent situation. These are the crucial points of mental hygiene. I am still at it. But, this time, on a much deeper level, much deeper. I don't work on the psychological level anymore. It is biology, today.

Now, about the communists: I was never a communist in the usual sense. *I was never a political communist.* I would like to have that fully on record. Never. Oh, yes, I worked in the organization. I worked with them.[2] I believed that capitalism was bad, but I don't believe, today, that the misery stems from capitalism. The misery is older than capitalism. I tried hard to get psychology, especially psychoanalytic psychology, into sociology. And I succeeded. I don't say that I did it all, of course.

[1] See letter from Reich to the publishers and editors of the *International Journal for Psychoanalysis*, p. 155.
[2] "In the years 1928 to 1930, I went into the communist-socialist camp to do practical field work in mental hygiene. I introduced the concept of neurosis and genital misery into social thinking. My first steps in this field resulted in the conclusion that, though the ideals of the movement were right, the techniques used to achieve the end were inadequate if not thoroughly ghastly. Accordingly, I embarked on improving the leftist movement for freedom by introducing psychiatric basic concepts into political sociology.
From the point of view of later developments of misery for myself and my beloved ones, I wished I had never started my program of improving the socialist movements. No more deadly enemies, no greater danger to my life and liberty or happiness have ever come than that movement directed by liberators without knowledge of the laws of responsible freedom. From the standpoint of learning, I would do it again, in spite of the heartbreak." Reich. From the Archives of the Orgone Institute.

Bernfeld began it about 1925, but he dropped it. I continued in 1927. In Austria, I worked with the communists, but I was in the Arbeiter Hilfe.[3] In Germany, I belonged to the socialist physicians under Simmel.[4] I worked with the communist faction because of the new laws in Russia—the sexual laws.[5] Freud was all for it. Today, everybody is for it except the Russians, who dropped it long ago. Somehow, the world has split up. You see, there was this tendency in the late twenties to unite psychology and Marxism, or psychoanalysis and Marxism.[6]

[3] "The Arbeiterhilfe (Worker's Help) consisted mainly of people who were not party members but sympathized openly with the Russian revolution. The Arbeiterhilfe and the 'Rote Hilfe' (Red Help) were designed as a kind of Red Cross organization. However, these affiliates consisting of non-political members were in many cases abused for political power purposes in the early thirties, without the consent or even the knowledge of the members of these organizations." Reich. From the Archives of the Orgone Institute.

[4] Ernst Simmel (1882-1947), president of the Society for Socialist Physicians in Berlin, who pioneered in the development of hospital care of patients, using psychoanalytic principles.

[5] "Lenin, as early as December 19 and 20, 1917, issued two relevant decrees. One was 'About the dissolution of marriage' . . . The other was, 'About civil marriage, children and the registration of marriage.' Both laws deprived the husband of his prerogatives of domination in the family, gave the woman the complete right to economic and sexual determination and declared it to be a matter of course that the woman could freely determine her name, domicile and citizenship.

". . . Divorce was made very easy. A sexual relationship which was considered a 'marriage' could be as easily dissolved as it had been established. The only criterion was mutual agreement among the partners.

". . . The registration of a relationship was not mandatory. Even when a relationship was registered, sexual relationships with others were 'not prosecuted'. However, not telling the partner about another relationship was considered 'fraud'. The obligation to pay alimony was considered only a 'transition measure'. The obligation lasted six months after the separation and only if the partner was unemployed or otherwise incapable of making a living." Reich, *The Sexual Revolution*, pp. 166-167.

[6] "People began to feel, in the middle of the 1920's, that with Sigmund Freud something crucial had happened in human society. As Wilhelm Reich expressed it in one of his books: Sexuality became aware of itself in the person of Sigmund Freud, just as economy began to be aware of itself in the person of Karl Marx. The trend in Europe to unite Freud and Marx

DR. EISSLER

Yes.

DR. REICH

But it fell apart. Russia degenerated. Communistic Marxism degenerated into Stalinism and imperialism. Freud is in the United States—I mean, psychology and all that. Is that clear?

DR. EISSLER

Yes.

DR. REICH

Now, they are opposed to each other, i.e., the economistic view and the study of human structure, human biology. That is how I see it. These were the subjects of the discussions with Freud. We agreed that the economic approach alone cannot solve the issue. It is very important, of course, that the people do not go hungry, that they have their food, that they have their shelters, that they have security. But that doesn't solve the problem of human structure or character formation. What you have to do is to first have your secure economic base and then go ahead and change human structure. Here, we were in complete agreement. And Freud was awfully enthusiastic about it. To him, it appeared as something very important. But then Federn came along. He was a Modju. Federn was a psychoanalytic Modju. He was very unhappy in his marriage, but he was a very, very good husband. He stuck to her and so on. And he was a "culturist." He used to read Goethe to his patients.

---

began to prevail in about 1927. At that time, nobody had an inkling of the future split of a mechanized and ruined Karl Marx who would be confined to an imperialist, Russian, tyrant state, and a badly mauled Freud confined to the USA, appearing frequently in a commercial manner as thousands of 'lay psychotherapists'." Reich, 1952. From the Archives of the Orgone Institute.

DR. EISSLER

His wife had an influence on him?

DR. REICH

I don't know. I always had a feeling that he was a very alive human being, too. It was always the same story. The man was alive, the woman was somehow out. The men gave into them, and they were then jealous or inimical to those who didn't give in.

When did you enter the psychoanalytic movement?

DR. EISSLER

Well, I went to psychoanalytic lectures from 1931 on.

DR. REICH

Are you a member of the psychoanalytic society now?

DR. EISSLER

Yes.

DR. REICH

In New York?

DR. EISSLER

Yes.

DR. REICH

May I ask you a question? Did you discuss this interview with anyone of the Board of Directors of the Psychoanalytic?

DR. EISSLER

What do you mean—discuss?

DR. REICH

Discuss what we should talk about?

DR. EISSLER
One or two, I think, know that I planned to interview you.

DR. REICH
Who?

DR. EISSLER
I think I told Hartmann and Kronold.

DR. REICH
You know Kronold was my student.

DR. EISSLER
Yes.

DR. REICH
He is quite decent, but they all left me. They all abandoned me.

DR. EISSLER
But they say you are a very good analyst.

DR. REICH
Yes. Other psychoanalysts don't know about this interview? They don't ask? But they know that I cooperate with you?

DR. EISSLER
Yes, sure. But their interest is really a peripheral one.

DR. REICH
Is that so?

DR. EISSLER
Yes.

DR. REICH
You know what I mentioned yesterday about that original dam-

age done to the human, to infants. That's what it is—this lack of interest. *Nobody is interested. They can't be interested. The protoplasm doesn't sparkle any more.* Oh, we encounter that everywhere. We have it right in our own midst. It is everywhere, everywhere. Were there any objections to my depositing the documents?

DR. EISSLER

Oh, no.

DR. REICH

There are a few severe enemies in the psychoanalytic association. Nunberg is very severe.[7] There are very many friends there, too, but they don't touch it. You know what I mean. They don't touch it.

Tell me, are people aware that wherever organizational development of Freud's science ran one way, its scientific development went another way?

DR. EISSLER

No, I don't think that people are aware of that.

DR. REICH

Aren't they? Aren't they? You see—I don't know whether you are quite aware of what I mean. Do you know who has kept the libido theory alive and working today? And who developed it? I regard myself as the only one who did it. Nobody else. Is that clear? I want this quite clearly on record. I claim that. I am not a

---

[7] "Freud, Sachs, Nunberg, Deutsch, Alexander and most other analysts refused to accept my concept of the psycho-economic and therapeutic significance of genitality. Freud's *Introductory Lectures on Psychoanalysis*, published as late as 1933, do not even mention the problem of the genital orgasm; nor does Nunberg's *Neurosenlehre.*" *Character Analysis*, p. 300.

psychoanalyst.[8] I am not interested in psychoanalysis. I have
no animosity against it. I have no grudge against it—not at all.
It is all cold and dead. But one thing is clear, and that I think
we should work out here. It was also a point of frequent discussion with Freud. I refer here to the relationship of the quantitative to the qualitative. To him, it was one of his greatest discoveries that an idea is not active on its own, but because it has a
certain energy cathexis, i.e., it has a certain amount of energy
attached to it. In this, he had brought the quantitative and the
qualitative together. He did the same thing when he claimed
that the neurosis had a somatic nucleus. But the quantitative,
the energy angle, was only a concept. It was not reality. Now,
whereas the psychoanalytic organization developed the qualitative angle, i.e., the ideas, their interconnection, and so on, I
picked up the energy angle. I had to hold on to the libido theory, you understand, not only because it was true, but because I
needed it. I needed it as a tool. It led into the physiological
realm. That means that what Freud called libido was not a
chemical,[9] but a movement of the protoplasm. Can you follow
me?

[8] "I have no objections whatsoever to anyone linking up Freud's ideational
concepts on the psychic energy with my discovery. I have done so myself.
However, I must guard against any attempt to write me down in history as
a Freudian or as one of the many psychotherapeutic schools which sprang
from the deletion of the living nerve of the Freudian theory, namely, the
libido theory. The actual discovery of the cosmic energy has nothing whatever to do with Freud. It is solely *my* responsibility, and I have to be on
guard since the consequences of this discovery are so very grave, resting on
my shoulders only." Reich, 1956. From the Archives of the Orgone Institute.
[9] "We know that the mechanisms of the psychoses are in essence no different from those of the neuroses, but we do not have at our disposal the
quantitative stimulation necessary for changing them. The hope of the
future here lies in organic chemistry or the access to it through endocrinology. This future is still far distant, but one should study analytically every
case of psychosis because this knowledge will one day guide the chemical
therapy." Sigmund Freud, in a letter to Marie Bonaparte, January 15, 1930.

DR. EISSLER
Yes.

DR. REICH

If an amoeba wants to go out toward something, it stretches out.
Right? If it is afraid, what does it do? It withdraws. It goes into
itself. Right? Now, that was the libido theory as I developed it
as a real, physiological function. And out of this came the discovery of the orgone energy.[1]

Now, I have to say a few words here: I don't think there are
many analysts who appreciate Freud's great achievement, the
discovery of a psychic energy. I don't think there are many who
know what that means. I said yesterday why they don't. Very
few have natural scientific training or the capacity to think in a
natural scientific way. I don't mean just psychological thinking.
It is much more. Freud was a natural scientist in that sense. He
thought in terms of quantity, energy, libido cathexis to ideas.
That is where the psychoanalytic organization fell completely
short, completely short. And that is where I hooked on. That is
what I owe to Freud in the discovery of the Life Energy.[2] What

---

Published in *The Life and Work of Sigmund Freud*, Vol. III, p. 449, by
Ernest Jones.
[1] "The basic question of all biology is that of the origin of the internal impulses of the living organism. Nobody doubts the fact that the difference
between the living and the non-living lies in the internal origin of the
motor impulses. This internal impulse can be due only to an energy at work
within the organism." *The Cancer Biopathy*, pp. 24-25.
It is this energy, originally discovered in 1939 in a culture of "bions,"
(microscopically visible vesicles of functioning energy) which Reich named
"orgone," a term derived from the words "organism" and "orgastic" to
indicate "the history of its discovery, namely, through the orgasm formula,
as well as its biological effect (of charging organic substances)." Ibid.,
p. 78.
[2] In a later notation, Reich suggested that "all ideas of energy, stasis and
discharge came from Breuer [Dr. Josef Breuer, Freud's original collaborator],
the sex point from Freud."

Freud called libido inside the organism is a reality outside the organism as well. You can see it on the devices.[3] That blue outside is orgone energy.[4] It is a reality. It was discovered on the basis of Freud's original libido, on the basis of the principle of energy. In my discussions with Freud, the problem of the content and the cathexis, the relationship of the idea and the quantity of energy attached to it were crucial points. The sexual angle was important because the genital excitation is the best example of that energy. When the penis erects, something physical happens. So I did not keep at the libido theory because I am an especial adherent of sex in the usual sense of the word, but because it was a natural scientific principle of energy quantity and objective functioning. I don't even feel myself to be a student of Freud any more. I have had nothing to do with him for a long time. I would even have much reason to be very angry at him.

[3] The microscope, telescope, orgonoscope, temperature-difference apparatus, electroscope, field meter, fluorophotometer, Geiger-Müller counter are some of the devices used to visualize and otherwise demonstrate and measure quantitatively the orgone energy in biological specimens and in the atmosphere.

[4] "*Blue is the specific color of orgone energy within and without the organism.* Classical physics tries to explain the blueness of the sky by the scattering of the blue and of the spectral color series in the gaseous atmosphere. However, it is a fact that blue is the color seen in all functions which are related to the cosmic or atmospheric or organismic orgone energy:

"*Protoplasm* of any kind, in every cell or bacterium is blue. It is generally mistaken as 'refraction' of light which is wrong, since the same cell under the same conditions of light loses its blueness when it dies.

"Thunder clouds are deeply blue, due to high orgone charges contained in the suspended masses of water.

"A *completely darkened room*, if lined with iron sheet metal (the so-called 'Orgone Room'), is not black, i.e., free of any light, but bluish or bluish-gray. Orgone energy luminates spontaneously; it is 'luminescent.'

"*Water* in deep lakes and in the ocean is blue.

"The color of luminating, decaying wood is blue; so are the luminating tail ends of glowworms, St. Elmo's fire, and the aurora borealis.

"The lumination in *evacuated tubes charged with orgone energy* is blue." Reich, *The Orgone Energy Accumulator—Its Scientific and Medical Use* (Orgone Institute Press, 1951), p. 15.

He didn't behave very well in 1933 and 1934 when I was in trouble, in great trouble. While I defended his work, he didn't want to support me. He refused.[5] But that has no bearing, whatsoever, on the factual, scientific angle of the whole thing. It is the quantitative factor, the energy principle that I owe to Freud, and it is that principle that separates me from the psychoanalysts. *Psychoanalysis is a psychology of ideas*, while *orgonomy is a science of physical energy*—physical energy inside the organism and outside the organism. Do I formulate it so that even one who is not in it can understand what it is all about?

DR. EISSLER

Yes.

DR. REICH

The libido which Freud talked about hypothetically and which he suggested might be chemical in nature is a concrete energy, something very concrete and physical. It is in the air and can be concentrated in an orgone energy accumulator.[6] I shall give you a pamphlet on it.[7] You have heard about it?

DR. EISSLER

Yes.

DR. REICH

So it is not psychoanalysis. It has nothing to do with psychoanalysis. But the psychoanalytic libido theory, the psychic en-

---

[5] See letters, pp. 158, 176.
[6] A means of collecting and concentrating the atmospheric orgone energy by a certain arrangement of organic and metallic materials, based on the observable fact that the former absorbs and the latter reflects this energy.
[7] *The Orgone Energy Accumulator—Its Scientific and Medical Use*. This was among the works of Reich that were physically destroyed by the Food and Drug Administration.

ergy theory, was a certain decisive step in the discovery which I made.[8]

Now, I would like to be sure that I do not give the impression that I try to depreciate or to debunk the psychoanalysts. I don't. As I told you, I am not at all interested in psychoanalysis. What I am interested in is how the Life Energy, which is in you and outside of you, works in you and through you upon the world. For instance, how does it work through you as a psychoanalyst upon your patient? What automatically works in you is what I call bio-energy. It is concrete. Libido, however, was only a term for a concept. Life Energy is something you can hear in the laboratory. You can hear it click on instruments. That is the significance of the transition from the libido theory to the concrete physical energy. What I am interested in is how this energy, which is outside in nature and is inside you and works through you, influences your patient. *If, as a psychoanalyst, that energy in you is thwarted, frustrated genitally, then your whole thinking system will be different from the person in whom it is not thwarted.* The way you look at the world and the way you see it will be different. Here, we are speaking again of the "genital character" and the "neurotic character." *In the genital character, this energy, this objective, cosmic energy works freely.* It flows freely. It is in contact. *In a neurotic character, it is*

8 "The emphasis which I have put upon Freud's libido theory, as a hypothetical forerunner of the actual discovery of the cosmic life energy, is due to the fact that, as a psychoanalyst, I worked practically and clinically with it for twelve years, and thus, arrived at my own discovery in the course of developments and conflicts within the psychoanalytic movement. However, I could have developed my discovery of the life energy as well from Driesch's 'Entelechy' or Bergson's 'Elan Vital', or from any of the biochemical branches of science, had I happened to have worked practically in any of these fields. Similar conflicts would have arisen to free my thoughts. This is to say that there are many forerunners of my discovery." Reich, 1954. From the Archives of the Orgone Institute.

thwarted and blocked. Now, whether the psychoanalyst is, or to what extent he is, a neurotic character determines how he looks upon my work. It will determine whether he slanders me or not, whether he thinks I am a psychopath, or whether he thinks I am a very normal and gay individual, or an individual who is outgoing and natural, and so on. You understand my point? I am not interested in these disturbances of the psychoanalysts for themselves, or because they did this or that to me. I am only interested in what manner they are thwarted and frustrated because *the distortion of the life force in the psychoanalysts was responsible for the degeneration of Freud's work.* Is that clearly formulated now?

DR. EISSLER

Yes.

DR. REICH

That is what I am interested in. The same distortion of the life force has taken place in all movements—in the Christian movement, the Marxist movement, in any movement, you understand. However, what is significant in psychoanalysis is that Freud was the first to touch upon the life energy hypothetically. He was the first to touch upon it, although only as a concept. Before him it was only surmised. It was only an idea, like the entelechy. But Freud, with his penetrating statement of a psychic energy principle, touched upon the life energy in the organism as an actual concept. Now, that is where I come in. Is that clear? From there, it developed right into the cosmic energy, measurable on the Geiger counter, visible in the blue of the atmosphere. That's why it is important whether a psychoanalyst smears my name or whether he knows what I am doing. If he smears my name, he is just sick. There is thwarted life energy in him. He tries to do to my work what he did to Freud's work by destroying the libido theory. Are the psychoanalysts aware that the libido theory is dead in their organization? [See Editors' Preface.]

DR. EISSLER

No, I don't think so. Most of them I think would not admit that.

DR. REICH

They would not admit that?

DR. EISSLER

I don't think so.

DR. REICH

There is no doubt about that. Think of an article like Sterba's on my work in which he leaves out the crucial orgasm question entirely. Oh, yes, I know they talk of anal and oral and so on. That is not the point, you understand. The point is the grasping of what the libido theory meant. *With the libido theory, psychology hooked onto natural science for the first time in the history of science.* I don't know whether or not you are really grasping it.

DR. EISSLER

Yes.

DR. REICH

You do. You understand that, until Freud, psychology was something beyond natural science. It still is for many, for most. And what I am telling you now is quite crucial. For the first time in the history of the human race, the mind was hooked up, at least theoretically, with nature at large. Do I make myself clear now?

Yes.

DR. REICH

That is where I come in. I made it *real* [9] through the discovery of the orgone energy. And that is why I say the libido theory is dead. Nothing happened to it. Nobody did anything with it. Talking about oral and anal things does not mean libido theory. To Freud, libido theory was, as you can see from "Beyond the Pleasure Principle" and such papers, something very basic and very deep. And, here, a part of his tragedy sets in. Here, also, was his interest in my work. He knew that I was scientifically minded, i.e., basically oriented toward fundamental natural processes. *The genital functioning in a person is an expression of his life energy.* If that is disturbed, as is the case in the average

---

[9] "What psychoanalytic theory calls 'id' is in reality the physical orgone function in the biosystem. The term 'id' expresses, in a metaphysical manner, the fact that there is in the biosystem a 'something' the functions of which are determined *outside* of the individual. *This 'something,' the 'id', is a physical reality; the cosmic orgone energy.* The living 'orgonotic system,' the 'bio-apparatus,' represents nothing but a special state of concentrated orgone energy. In a recent review, a psychoanalyst described the 'orgone' as 'identical with Freud's id.' This is as correct as the contention, say, that the 'entelechy' of Aristotle and Driesch is identical with the 'orgone'. It is true, indeed, that the terms 'id,' 'entelechy', 'elan vital' and 'orgone' describe 'the same thing.' But one makes things all too easy for oneself with such analogies. *'Orgone' is a visible, measurable and applicable energy of a cosmic nature.* Such concepts as 'id', 'entelechy', or 'elan vital', on the other hand, are only the expression of *inklings* of the existence of such an energy. Are the 'electromagnetic waves' of Maxwell 'the same' as the 'electromagnetic waves' of Hertz? Undoubtedly they are. But with the latter one can send messages across the oceans while with the former one cannot.

"Such 'correct' equations without a mention of the *practical* differences serve the function of verbalizing away great discoveries in natural science. They are as unscientific as the sociologist who, in a recent review, referred to the orgone as a 'hypothesis.' With hypotheses, with such things as the 'id' or 'entelechy', one cannot charge blood corpuscles or destroy cancer tumors; with orgone energy, one can." *Character Analysis,* p. 304.

psychoanalyst, he doesn't function, and he can't think in the bio-energetic way. He can't think in that direction. *And he hates.* Now, that is the background for the hate, for the slander that came my way.

DR. EISSLER

Do you think that Freud abandoned the libido theory?

DR. REICH

No. Never! Never! Only he couldn't find his way further. He was stuck. I believe the way was my way, the way I went so successfully. I had to go through character analysis, the emotions, the pleasure anxieties, the opposite directions of flow of bio-energy in the organism, from there to the plasmatic movement—yes, to the amoeba—and, then, into the orgone energy outside. *Libido as a physical cosmic reality—that is my work.* Freud provided the concept. This is where he came in. This, to my mind, was his greatest deed. He was a very great man, a very great man.

POSTSCRIPT

*This letter from the Archives of the Orgone Institute was writ-
ten after the completion of the interview. It was addressed to
Dr. Eissler, but not sent.*

Dear Dr. Eissler:

The delivery of this interview has been delayed because I
wished to finish reading the first volume of the Sigmund Freud
biography by Ernest Jones. This reading has shown me that the
following additions should be filed with the Archives:

(1) In the interview, I had characterized Sigmund Freud as
an animal in a cage, the cage being only his environment and his
pupils. The Jones biography reveals the fact that it was, in addition, Sigmund Freud himself who held on to his own imprisonment by Jewish customs and beliefs which, in the intellectual
sphere, he loathed.

(2) In the interview, I had offered the opinion that Sigmund
Freud was a genitally healthy man. The biography reveals what

I had not known, that he suffered, under familial and religious pressures, from severe sexual stasis during the nearly five years of his frustrating betrothal to a girl who, quite obviously, was deeply spellbound by a neurotic mother. This might seem unimportant had it not forced Sigmund Freud to hamper all further developments concerning genitality. Freud seemed to have been stuck in his own need to "sublimate" which he, then, made valid for all by translating it into a wrong psychological theory. Contemporaries of his such as Strindberg, Ibsen, Nietzsche, who had no fear, were far ahead of Freud in these matters.

(3) Sigmund Freud's personal background also explains why he behaved the way he did in the reception of my orgasm theory. It explains, also, why he was so inimical to America where the sexual revolution was born from the genital frustrations and realizations of the early pioneers who liked female companionship. Freud could not possibly accept such realizations without changing his whole being.

(4) I also did not know that Sigmund Freud had been on the way to the discovery of the bio-energy in clinical activity (see Jones' account of the "Project Manuscript" [1]) which he later rejected. Freud had missed the discovery of the physical life energy as he had missed completing his cocaine studies. All this, because of the severe inhibition imposed by a Jewish family and a Jewish bride upon his very alive and emotionally longing bio-system. This tragic aspect of Sigmund Freud's background is clearly manifested in and explains what I had, to begin with, emphasized as the great despair in his facial expression. His psychological discoveries, great and crucial as they were, thus demonstrates a *run-away* from the full realization of those aspects of his discovery which I had, for a decade, pursued in the name of

[1] *The Life and Work of Sigmund Freud*, Vol. I, pp. 379-395.

Freud, but, later, had to shoulder myself when he refused to acknowledge their simple consequences as explained in my orgasm theory.[2]

WILHELM REICH, M. D.

Orgonon

Rangeley, Maine

[2] "I took the responsibility for Freud, that is for things Freud did not want." Reich, in a telephone conversation with Dr. Eissler, March 26, 1952.

PART 2 DOCUMENTARY
SUPPLEMENT

EXPLANATORY NOTE

Although, during the early 1930's, Reich still believed in the basic scientific nature of Marxism, he had recognized "the tremendous gap between sex-economic sociology and vulgar economism." As early as 1932, his writings were being banned by socialist and communist organizations, and he was even threatened with execution if Marxism should gain power in Germany. He was expelled from communist organizations because he had introduced sexology into sociology and pointed out its implications for human structure. Between 1934 and 1937, all of his writings were banned in the U.S.S.R.

The Marxist terminology which appears in this correspondence was deleted from the later editions of his early works. As to his relationship to Marxist organizations, Reich, later, had this to say: "I do not regret my many years' work as a physician in Marxist organizations. I owe my sociological knowledge not to books, but primarily to the practical experience of the struggles on the part of the masses for a decent, free existence. The best sex-economic insights, in fact, were gained as a result of the *errors* in thinking on the part of the masses, the errors which brought them the fascist pestilence. To me as a physician, the working individual, with his everyday concerns, was accessible in a way he never is to a party politician. The party politician saw only the 'worker's class' which he was going to 'fill with class consciousness.' I saw the living being, man, as he was living under social conditions of the worst kind, conditions which he had created himself, which, characterologically anchored, he carried within him and from which he tried in vain to free himself. The chasm between economistic and biosociological conceptions became unbridgeable. The theory of the 'class individual' became replaced by the knowledge of the irrational nature of the society formed by the animal, man.

". . . Dialectic materialism as outlined by Engels in his *Anti-Dühring* developed into *biophysical functionalism*. This development was made possible by the discovery of the biological energy, the orgone (1936–1939). Sociology and psychology were put on a solid biological foundation. Such a development cannot remain without influence on thought. As thinking develops, old concepts change and new concepts take the place of obsolete ones. The Marxist 'consciousness' was replaced by '*dynamic structure*,' 'needs' by 'orgonotic instinctual processes,' 'tradition' by 'biological and characterological rigidity,' etc.

". . . Does that mean that the economic theory of Marxism is fundamentally wrong? I should like to clarify this question by an illustration. Is the microscope of Pasteur's time, or Leonardo da Vinci's water pump 'wrong'? Marxism is a scientific economic theory which stems from the social conditions of the early 19th century. However, the social process did not stand still, but developed into the fundamentally different process of the 20th century. In this *new*-social process, it is true, we find all the basic elements of the 19th century, just as in the modern microscope we find the basic structure of that of Pasteur, and in the modern plumbing system the basic principle of Leonardo's pump. But one, like the other, would be of no use to us today. They have been surpassed by fundamentally new processes and functions which correspond to fundamentally new concepts and techniques. The Marxist parties in Europe failed and declined because they tried to comprehend fascism of the 20th century, a fundamentally new phenomenon, with concepts belonging to the 19th century. They declined as social organizations because they failed to keep alive the developmental possibilities inherent in any scientific theory." [1]

[1] From the Preface to the third edition of *The Mass Psychology of Fascism* (New York: Orgone Institute Press, 1946).

1) C O R R E S P O N D E N C E*

(*Reich to Adler*)[1]

Vienna, March 10, 1920

SEMINAR FOR SEXOLOGY

My dear Doctor:

Your lecture on the "Foundations of Individual Psychology" at the Society for Social Medicine prompts me to write you on a subject which has long been on my mind and which has provoked lively discussions in our seminar.

In full appreciation of and admiration for your doctrines of ego psychology—or rather, just because of this—I could not dismiss certain rising doubts, not about their *validity* but about their *comprehensive applicability, especially to the field of neu-*

---

* Unless otherwise noted, all material in this section was translated from the German by Therese Pol.
[1] This letter was written while Reich was a medical student at the University of Vienna.

roses and perversions. So if I take the above-mentioned lecture as a vehicle for discussion, it is done because the case histories you presented from your practice lend themselves to illustrations of my argument.

I will not touch on everything but will confine myself to those points which seem to me in greatest need of clarification. If I did not state these objections at the end of your lecture (motion for discussion submitted by colleague Hartmann), it was, among other things, because I know from experience that such discussions, especially when only a brief fifteen minutes is allotted to them, are usually unproductive.

1. I am completely mystified as to what motivated you, in a lecture plumbing the depths of individual psychology and touching on the problems of almost every aspect of our emotional life, to neglect the *sexual phenomenon* to the point of not even mentioning it, even though, in my opinion, the latter exerts at least as much influence over our emotional life as those elements which (in the adult) rightly play an important role (will to power, instinct of self-preservation). Or am I to understand that the final case you mentioned—the girl who did not want to get married (I shall revert to this below)—contains the germ of an explanation, namely, that even sexuality is subject to the "will to power"? I shall further on elucidate the nature of the doubts—more than that, the reasoned objections—which make this explanation unacceptable to me.—

2. I visualize the extent of the importance which you attribute to the will to power and its final directional goal for the emotional life of the individual and his position in the community; I acknowledge the struggle between it and the community of feelings innate to all of us, as it takes place *in the adult* at the

height of his individual development; but I definitely feel that your exposition about the *first beginnings*, the most *primitive germinations* contains certain ambiguities. I feel that the analysis of the emotional stirrings attending this will to power, their synthesis into a virtually tangible form of the mechanism of the will—striving, surpassing others, extolling one's own personality (ambition)—is completely successful. But your explanation of its *autogenesis* starts at a stage which surely cannot be the point of origin. For if this will to power originated from the desire to become like the father (reinforced by the [inferiority] feeling that this cannot be done), the explanation would suffice if we did not have to ask ourselves: in what respect does the four-year-old boy want to become like his father? If he feels the stirrings of inferiority, this must have a cause—and what is it? However, our curiosity will scarcely be satisfied by this answer: the youngster wants to become an engineer or a shoemaker like his father; he wants to build equally fine houses, etc., and since he cannot do this, his inferiority feelings awaken, and along with them the will to surpass his father. We can even occasionally observe that little boys show preference for games imitating the occupations of adults, the closest model being the father. But we will have to say that this is not always the case, and if it does happen, it is frequently an imitation, free of envy, whose strongest motives must be sought in entirely different areas. We should even admit that nothing could be more alien to the child than the reality, burdened with worries and sorrow, which in the long run cannot be concealed from him, particularly if he is intelligent; that he will select from this *reality* only that which gives him the most *pleasure*—that is, only the marvelous freedom, the come-and-go-as-you-please, above all the freedom from the paternal whip that keeps coercing him back into the narrow circle he

Sigmund Freud. The photograph is inscribed (in German):
"To Dr. Wilh. Reich as kind remembrance of Sigm Freud.
March 1925."

everything else. But she was utterly exhausted. Freud, on the other hand, although he said he had nearly perished, was rather triumphant at having single-handed defeated his enemy without any help from her, and the hurricane blew itself out. How the remaining difficulties in the way of the marriage were overcome will be related presently.

In reading through the tremendous story I have outlined here one apprehends above all how mighty were the passions that animated Freud and how unlike he was in reality to the calm scientist he is often depicted. He was beyond doubt someone whose instincts were far more powerful than those of the average man, but whose repressions were even more potent. The combination brought about an inner intensity of a degree that is perhaps the essential feature of any great genius. He had been torn by love and hate before, and was to be again more than once, but this was the only time in his life— when such emotions centered on a woman—that the volcano within was near to erupting with destructive force.

[handwritten note: Freud was simply love starved, like a steam engine before explosion —]

See page 58 for an explanation of the notations on Reich's copy of *The Life and Work of Sigmund Freud.*

VIII

Marriage

(1 8 8 6)

FREUD WAS NOT ONLY MONOGAMIC IN A VERY UNUSUAL DEGREE, BUT FOR a time seemed to be well on the way to becoming uxorious. But just as after a time he recognized that his love "was passing from its lyric phase into an epic one," [1] so he was realist enough to know that a happy marriage would be less tempestuous than the emotional period that preceded it. "Society and the law cannot in my eyes bestow on our love more gravity and benediction than it already possesses. . . . And when you are my dear wife before all the world and bear my name we will pass our life in calm happiness for ourselves and earnest work for mankind until we have to close our eyes in eternal sleep and leave to those near us a memory every one will be glad of." [2] A wish that was wholly fulfilled, but a rather unusual one to express in the first weeks of an engagement.

He had already informed her that she must expect to belong entirely to his family and no longer to her own. So the statement he quoted from Meynert a year later that "the first condition in every marriage should be the right to expel one's in-laws" seems to have been a one-sided one.

Mostly, however, his picture of their future was drawn in a lighter vein. "All we need is two or three little rooms where we can live and eat and receive a guest and a hearth where the fire for cooking does not go out. And what things there will have to be: tables and chairs, beds, a mirror, a clock to remind the happy ones of the passage of time, an armchair for an hour of agreeable day-dreaming, carpets so that the *Hausfrau* can easily keep the floor clean, linen tied up in fancy ribbons and stored on their shelves, clothes of the newest cut and hats with artificial flowers, pictures on the wall, glasses for the

139

Reich in Davos, Switzerland, February 1927. The inscription reads: "Conflict with Freud."

Davos, March 1927.

Sletten, Denmark, 1934.

In his laboratory, 1944.

At Orgonon, Rangeley, Maine, 1950. On the back of the photograph Reich wrote: "Still in doubt about whether to fight EP [Emotional Plague] on its own ground."

The Orgone Energy Observatory at Orgonon. The building is now maintained as the Wilhelm Reich Museum.

Reich's study in the observatory at Orgonon.

The study and library at Orgonon. The paintings are by Reich.

Laboratory in the observatory at Orgonon.

Reich's tomb at Orgonon. The bust is by Jo Jenks, 1949.

tries to break by every available means. And, here, alone, we would find the relation you have emphasized: cause—effect, pressure by the father (by all education)—inferiority feeling (and the will to surpass the father, i.e., *to overcome him, to be free of him*).

But when we pursue our investigations, we soon come upon the inexorable truth that the final meaning of our sexual life is invariably the ultimate and highest pleasure, and that in children we find pleasure-directed actions which in adults are known as perversions; that, for example, we cannot describe the child's unquestionably pleasurable voyeurism and exhibitionism as anything but sexual (we have no reasonable grounds for not doing so); that, furthermore, since the child subscribes to the pleasure principle, it frequently takes great efforts to bring him back to the reality function inhibiting his need for pleasure, but that the sexual instincts belong to the former and the ego instincts to the latter principle; and that in the *final analysis* and *primarily* (I am not claiming, exclusively) the inferiority feeling has its origin in the *sexual (pleasure) intimidation by the father*, which is needed for the gradual integration of the child into cultural community life. —Now if *one* infantile root of the will to power might be found in the inferiority feeling caused by sexual intimidation—(to avoid any misunderstandings *ab ovo*, let me emphasize that I would never think of shifting this source of the will to power to the adult personality)—then I would like to mention another which was omitted in your lecture: *sadism*. I would like to point to the enormously conspicuous circumstance that persons with a particularly highly developed will to power also show a distinctly sadistic character trait. Sadism is an indispensable tool of the will to power: in striving for his stated goal, the individual is not merely content with overtaking and surpassing his fellow beings, but he also endeavors to push them back and inflict harm; he is like a runner who will trip up his rivals to secure his own victory. But that sadism has a sexual origin can scarcely be refuted in the face of sadistic *perversion*. Here I would like to remark that one of the most important mechanisms in the individual's development seems to me that process in which certain sexual impulses—mostly those which in their extreme forms constitute the *momentum movens* for the corresponding perversions—are shifted from the sexual constitution into the ego constitution (Freud: sublimation), where they find their gratification in forms which do justice to the ego without clashing with the demands of culture. Time and again we simultaneously find splinter products of these sublimated drives in the sexual constitution as, for example, in the sadistic trait of the male's sexual wooing. The impulse to usurp (?) with its more physical potentiality for gratification; its psychic correlate, the drive for knowledge (it is an established fact that the child's curiosity is primarily directed toward the mysterious, which is largely the sexual), major facets of the voyeuristic impulse, among others, gradually, with advancing development, are put into the service of the ego, and just here lie most of the guarantees against psychic illness in the individual.

If I finally add that, in my opinion, the "inferiority feeling" appears to be identical with the concept of the "castration complex" of Freud's school, only modified in that it is shifted to the ego constitution; if I further find that your explanation for case II (young man, second-eldest son, God-fearing, etc.) completely coincides with the psychoanalytic view on the regression of compulsion neurotics into the (anal-) sadistic phase, I am doing it in order to ask you to uncover any possible error in this view; the same goes for my perhaps erroneous assumption that you have isolated the *one* aspect of infantile development, namely, sexual intimidation (see castration complex), and have elaborated it far beyond general doctrines, assigning it in later life as "inferiority feeling" to the ego constitution as the foundation stone of ego psychology.—

Hence my questions might be summarized as follows:

a) What is your opinion on tracing the inferiority feeling back to *earlier* stages of development?

b) Is the inferiority feeling the expanded form of the castration complex, taken from the sexual constitution?

c) Is there any connection at all?

d) If not, then what is the first cause which generates the inferiority feeling?

3. *Case III: young girl, beauty; wants to get married but rejects all suitors.*

You explained that the girl did *not* want to get married because she refused to be oppressed and neglected like her mother had been. However, aside from a circumstance to be mentioned below, this contradicts the experience that can be observed hourly and daily: to wit, that the married state is the ideal for almost every woman unless she just has a masculine disposition; that every girl's most ardent wish is to have a husband; that, in contradistinction to your view, the passive and subordinate are inherent in the nature of the female; that the inferiority feeling of the average woman—and she alone can be considered in this context—is rooted in the chains imposed on her in *sexualibus* by basic cultural morality. But it is far more logical to interpret the traditional complaint of girls during puberty and later, "I'd give anything to be a boy!", to mean:

"Then I would have all the (sexual) freedom I want!", rather than: "Then I could do great things!" —For the road to social achievement is wide open to modern girls and women, and still the wish to be a man persists; quite apart from the fact that the average middle-class girl wants anything but a profession, while the proletarian girl has to work anyway, and would still rather be a man. Here the question arises as to why the absolutely and relatively greater inferiority feeling of the female sex does not produce, by way of overcompensation, a will to power far stronger than the man's. . . . In explaining this case, you mentioned the father's extraordinary love for his young daughter and later, it seemed to me, you did not refer to this very important circumstance again. Is it not likely, then, that the girl returned her father's love, could not emancipate herself from him and rejected all suitors, regardless of her wish to get married, which even seems to have tormented her?

Had she always articulated the conscious wish to be married? And how am I to interpret your explanation that she did *not* want to get married? The foundation for this diagnosis is lacking.

You stated yourself that the patient suffered from sexual conflicts, but you continued to attribute the cause of her illness to the will to power. The only possible conclusion: sexuality is subordinated to the will to power; but sexuality is demonstrably subordinated to the sexual drive which strives solely for *pleasure, and nothing else,* and not for power.

4. There is no question that a person who has set himself too high a goal owing to his overdeveloped will to power (case I), can be cured if he can be made to exchange it (which seldom works) for a deeper, more accessible goal (final cure). But can-

not such an individual also be cured if the *causes* of his ambition which are rooted in earliest childhood are disclosed to him (causal cure)?

I could add a few more comments, but this is probably more than enough and the other matters are of secondary importance.

Very respectfully yours,
(signed) WILHELM REICH,
Student of Medicine
IX Berggasse 7/16

(Reich to Ferenczi)[3]

Vienna, 11th February 1925

My dear Doctor:

Please accept my sincere apologies for taking up your valuable time with this letter, but the matter seems important enough to be submitted to you since you were a party to the conflict with *Adler*.

With the Professor's[4] consent, I am currently working on a book on psychoanalytic therapy and technique. It was originally intended for the Springer Verlag, but from the way it is shaping up it would be more suitable for a more restricted analytic circle. Now in casting the chapter on abbreviated methods ("active technique," etc.) I read your paper "Elaboration of the Active Technique" and found the following passages which I had previously overlooked: "Adler said that we should not concern ourselves with analyzing the libido but the 'nervous character' instead. My current propositions show certain analogies with these

[3] This is a fragment. It was not sent.
[4] Freud.

modifications, but the differences are many and conspicuous." And further: "The character investigations are never in the foreground of our technique, neither do they play the same decisive role as they do with Adler, but they are applied only if certain abnormal traits of a psychotic coloration interfere with the normal progress of the analysis." [5] Now I have made a special study of the psychoanalysis of the character, particularly in conjunction with "The Ego and the Id," and have summarized the partial results in a brief paper on the impulsive character which is soon to be published.[6] But the principal conclusion of this research, stimulated by "The Ego and the Id" concerning the character and its analysis, seems to me the, by now, generally accepted opinion that we are progressing from symptom analysis to a therapy that investigates the characterological foundations of the symptom neurosis; and that true and lasting cures can be achieved only if we succeed in modifying the neurotic character, which is the substructure of its symptomatology. (In the ego: overcoming ambivalence and narcissism; in the sexual sphere: building up the "erotic reality sense," the unambivalent, heterosexual genital libido.) The difficulty lies in circumscribing those analytic situations which do not belong to symptom but to character analysis. We are, however, getting closer to Adler's viewpoint, even if our character analysis differs substantially from his. It is only fair to admit this. This concession to Adler is sufficiently neutralized if we spell out the difference: *not* libido *but* character analysis (*Adler*) versus character analysis *through* analyzing the libido (*Freud*).—

Another difficulty is found in the addendum (1923) to the

[5] "I. Journal 1921, p. 248."
[6] *Der Triebhafte Charakter* (Leipzig, Vienna, Zurich: Internationaler psychoanalytischer Verlag, 1925).

complete edition,[7] Vol. VIII, p. 257 (Psychoanalysis of a phobia of a five-year-old boy). We read in the body of the text: "I cannot make up my mind whether to presuppose a separate aggressive instinct side by side with and equal to the sexual and the self-preservation instinct we know." And now the addendum: "The book was written at a time when Adler apparently was still rooted in the soil of psychoanalysis . . . Since then I, too, have been led to determine an aggressive instinct which is not identical with Adler's. I prefer to call it 'destructive' or death instinct . . ." Since "The Ego and the Id," we can no longer doubt that sadism—the aggressive, destructive death instinct—stands as the equal of Eros, and we are learning to assess its importance, which differs from Adler's in being less one-sided, and yet somehow resembling it. I must confess that the contradiction between text and addendum irritated me all the more as I felt that the Professor did not unequivocally resolve it; for what Adler *at the time* understood to be an aggressive instinct is the *same* that *Freud* calls destructive instinct. Freud's concept means just that and even more, namely, the biological basis (death instinct) of psychic aggression. If the tendency toward independent systems had not interfered, *Adler's* theory would have led directly to today's results *without* underestimating the libido. Adler's priority with respect to the core of his doctrine—and only the core—should be acknowledged, though always with a detailed exposition of the differences. I think that such a stand would be the best defense against the Adlerian "aggressive drive against psychoanalysis."

Or am I wrong? Is our destructive instinct really so radically different from Adler's? For years I have thoroughly studied

[7] Sigmund Freud, *Gesammelten Schriften* (Vienna, Zurich, Leipzig: Internationaler Psychoanalytischer Verlag, 1924).

Adler and the superficiality of his doctrine amid long discussions. But now I cannot dismiss the impression that the Adler of today, at least in some respects, is the victim of an injustice committed earlier. He had made an important discovery, but, like Rank, inflated its importance and . . .

(*Reich to Federn*)[8]

Vienna, February 12, 1926

My dear Doctor:

I believe my attitude in the outpatient clinic affair has shown that I do not allow my judgment of certain incidents to be obscured by petty personal feelings and that I know how to subordinate such matters to the more important interests of the Association and of the psychoanalytic movement. I must explicitly emphasize this with regard to what follows below. I felt—at first intuitively and later upon mature consideration—that the elimination of one of the two secretariat positions from the executive committee was a boycott of my person and a *completely undeserved* wrong. Here are the basic facts:

You will no doubt remember, my dear Doctor, that you personally advised me as early as the fall of 1923, when the executive committee met for reelection (Dr. Rank was then acting chairman), that my election was being considered for the office of second secretary but did not materialize because one of the

[8] This letter was not sent. Across the top of the letter appear the following notes in Reich's hand: "Nicht abgeschickt! Woch immer blind!—XII [Dec.] '34—Still blind, 1952." Under Federn's name appear the words: "The Pestilent Digger."

two secretaries was supposed to be a lay analyst (Dr. Bernfeld). As far as I know, you did not find a vestige of frustrated ambition on my part. I accepted the arguments.

On the occasion of the last election of secretaries, after you became acting chairman following Rank's resignation from the executive committee, you told me that I would have become secretary, along with Nunberg, if it had not been necessary to iron out certain differences with Jokl and to appoint him for political reasons. Nunberg was elected because he had seniority. (May I be permitted to remind you in this connection that I have seniority over Jokl.) I accepted these political arguments, too, even if I did not approve their specific political nature, and I, the "aggressive, paranoid and ambitious" type, forgot the whole affair without being in the least upset about it. It was only after the most recent decisions of the executive committee that both incidents assumed significance in my mind. Now the position of secretary was simply liquidated with the explanation that Bernfeld was the only one being considered *ad personam*. And what about the post of second secretary before Bernfeld's election?

Please believe me when I say that I thought of my automatic advancement to Bernfeld's position (as secretary or librarian) for the first time when you spoke of the new election in the board meeting.

I had a twofold interest in being on the executive committee. The first was motivated by the understandable desire to see and listen to the Professor more frequently. Infantile, perhaps, but neither ambitious nor criminal. The second was purely factual: I feel that for several years I have presented important suggestions which actually should have originated with a member of the executive committee since they concerned organizational questions such as establishing, conducting and developing the technical seminar (the chairmanship of which I have never claimed); differentiating between two kinds of members, systematizing the clinic services and the employment of physicians. (My admission as acting chairman to the executive committee of the clinic—an admission I did not claim but which was promised to me—suffered the same fate, for even flimsier reasons, as did my admission to the executive committee of the Association. Without bemoaning the former, I performed my duties in the outpatient clinic to the best of my ability and judgment, giving no cause for complaint, in spite of constant vexations.) Without my energetic efforts against the decision of the Association, the important question of the psychoanalytic specialist might not have been tackled for many years. My organizational work in the Association, combined with my scientific activity, gave me the feeling of *justified* expectation. To my mind, the fact that this expectation was not fulfilled is significant in one respect only (although, judging by past experiences, I must assume that the motives of basest ambition will be imputed to me): What does this boycott mean? I am unable to determine who started it. I only see a collective action of the executive committee. In the interest of my position in the Association it is my duty—for the present, to you alone—to list the reasons which I suspect are at the basis of this action.

My activity—which, like all positive things, also has its negative aspects—has earned me the reputation of being aggressive. I share this fate with Tausk. I had to admit that for a while, stung by an irrelevant scientific opposition and by the general conditions in the Association, I did not exercise sufficient restraint, a fact which I regretted very, very much, and, on realizing it, I changed my conduct immediately. However, I may safely say that, no matter in what defensive position I found myself, I never insulted a colleague or otherwise hurt his feelings. Should this nevertheless have happened, I am ready to make any amends that are asked for. I never intended any personal offense but always objectively said what I was convinced I was justified in saying—without false consideration, however, for age or position of the criticized party. I have always welcomed objective criticism. On the other hand, I have had to put up with many things that would have prompted any one among you to insist on an arbitration procedure, and yet I did not react personally (*coram publico* or in private) or aggressively. That my objective criticism became stricter still is something I cannot be blamed for. May I recall the personal insults of Dr. Hitschmann, Drs. Nunberg and Hoffer; also, the irrelevant personal criticism of my lectures by Dr. Reik ("The paper is good, but I would not like to have written it"). I will not even mention all the needling—so intangible, without being the less hurtful—that I cannot itemize without making a fool of myself.

Also, please do not ask me for details about colleagues (there is only one among them who is younger than I am) who are apparently well-intentioned toward me. Unless it can be proved that I made gross or numerous serious errors which would explain the attitude of many members and, by extension, the attitude of the executive committee, then only one explanation suggests itself: our Association is suffering from intramural envy. A paralyzing skepticism prevails; almost no one takes an active interest in the outpatient clinic, and anyone who wants to bring clarity to the controversial question of analytic therapy and refuses to become stifled in his interest in psychoanalysis as a science and movement is looked upon with a jaundiced eye.

A conversation with Professor Freud about analytic therapy convinced me that an infinite number of opinions, circulated as belonging to the Professor (e.g., on passivity), are either falsely attributed to him or, if he voiced them at all, have been misunderstood. Whence stems this shyness to discuss our therapy which is so dangerous for psychoanalysis as well as for the individual analysts? The idiotic rationalization is: the Professor does not think much of therapy. And yet, it is nothing but one's own inner insecurity and lack of sincerity which take cover behind Freud. I am not an optimist, as people keep telling me over and over. I am merely seeking the truth about our achievements, and for this purpose, confident of analytic honesty, I created the technical seminar. I have worked for many years to obtain insight into the circumstances of successful and unsucessful analyses. I interpret it as a symptom, and blame everyone who takes this personally, for letting me be the only one in the seminar, in courses and in publications who has reported on failures and tried to clarify these in common discussion. Most of the Viennese analysts report either on the theory of the case alone or on successful cases only.

So this is the crime that makes me unpopular: I criticized the ostrich attitude as being unanalytic; I publicly maintained that an analyst is duty-bound to discharge a patient when he has lost the thread of the analysis and is unable to find it again; he must deal with the therapeutic theory of each case and he must study the criteria for prognosis.

I have repeatedly asked for cooperation, and have met either with blind criticism or scorn for my efforts.

(signed) WILHELM REICH

(Reich to Freud)[1]

Vienna I

Neutorgasse 8

April 18, 1928

My dear Professor:

I am writing you, in your capacity as chairman of the Vienna Psychoanalytic Association, to complain about Dr. Paul Federn, acting chairman of the meetings.

In yesterday's meeting I lectured on "A Problem of Psychoanalytic Technique," reporting on the technique of dealing with narcissistic defense. Last summer, I was criticized for giving my technical lectures at the Seminar and not at the Association. In yesterday's lecture, I wished to present to the Association one of the problems which has been discussed for years at the Seminar, in order to elucidate the differences of opinion prevailing in the Seminar. To my greatest astonishment, Dr. Federn declared that what I had presented was so commonplace that it did not belong in the Association. This may be true or not; but I must protest against Dr. Federn's hateful, high-handed tone, and against the fact that he paralyzed the discussion by proposing that the points of contention should not be debated, which, in view of the Association's general apathy for debate, was quite enough. This unprofessional attitude of a chairman cannot, and must not, be tolerated.

It is not only my own feeling but the conviction of almost all analysts, particularly the younger ones, that Dr. Federn inhibits all constructive work by his inconsistency, his inability to conduct a discussion, and especially by his embarrassing manner of belittling everything a younger analyst may say; he is not only hampering the development of the Vienna Association but,

1 This letter was not sent.

worse, contributing to its deterioration. Dr. Sterba and Dr. Bibring, who, at my suggestion, were to present to the Association surveys on technique and therapy developed at the Seminar, have refused to do so because they do not want to expose themselves to Dr. Federn's supercilious condescension. If Dr. Federn complained last year that the Seminar draws off lectures from the Association, then he should not now brush aside everything the younger analysts have to say; even if their knowledge is rather basic, they still struggle to acquire it on their own because it is generally held that Dr. Federn's technical course was inadequate and did not offer what he calls "commonplace." The younger analysts dare not complain because they fear for their future. Conditions in the Association are utterly depressing. In view of my allegiance to the Association, my interest in the development of analysis which, in spite of the persistently hostile attitude of the public at large, is becoming socially acceptable, and because of the internal state of affairs, I am forced to bring this matter out into the open. I feel that, in this instance, personal considerations would only harm the work. Given these circumstances, active colleagues within the Association are bound to lose all pleasure in the scientific work.

Devotedly yours,
(signed) DR. REICH

To the
Publishers and Editors of the
International Journal for Psychoanalysis
Vienna

(n.d.)[2]

As publisher of the I.Z.f.Ps., Professor Freud has found it necessary to add the following comment[3] to my paper, "The Masochistic Character":

"Special circumstances have caused the publisher to direct the reader's attention to a point that is usually taken for granted. Within the framework of psychoanalysis this journal gives every author who submits a paper for publication full freedom of opinion, and in turn does not assume any responsibility for these opinions. In the case of Dr. Reich, however, the reader should be informed that the author is a member of the Bolshevist party. Now it is known that Bolshevism sets similar limits to scientific research as does a church organization. Party obedience demands that *everything contradicting the premises of its own dogma be rejected.*[4] It is up to the reader of this article to clear the author of such suspicions; the publisher would have made the same comment if he had been presented with a work of a member of the S.J. [Jesuits]"

The covering letter to the publisher emphasized that the paper could not appear if I did not consent to the above comment.[5] In principle, I would like to state the following in reference to this measure taken by Professor Freud:

[2] Written in 1932.
[3] Dated January 1, 1932.
[4] Underlined by Reich with the notation: "i.e., Freud's *dogma* of the death instinct."
[5] "Certain Berlin psychoanalysts opposed this procedure, and suggested instead that Reich's article should be published together with a reply. This was done. This 'reply' was written by Siegfried Bernfeld under the title

reflected an empirical-analytic approach, while the others presented philosophical hypotheses of a transparently bourgeois-reactionary kind. In spite of this, I do not deny that today, influenced by my Marxist philosophy, I am trying to comprehend psychoanalysis in the context of the total sociological picture.

5) In the past years, Professor Freud has never expressed an opinion on the accuracy or inaccuracy of my analytic theories. Neither has he explained just why he feels that my criticism of the doctrine of the death instinct is factually wrong.

(signed) WILHELM REICH

(Reich to Max Eitingon)

Berlin, October 14, 1932

To the Executive Committee of the
German Psychoanalytic Association
Attn: Dr. Eitingon
Berlin

My dear Doctor:

In our conversation of October 6th, you asked me not to admit any candidates in the first training stages to the unofficial technical seminar I am conducting, and to limit attendance to those analysts who at least are guests of the Association. You justified this demand by stating that I differ with Prof. Freud on the death instinct theory, which, judging by the latest decisions, has become an integral part of psychoanalytic theory. You left it to me to find a way of excluding such candidates and non-guests of the Association. I have not been able to follow through with your request. Since you officially opposed my election for membership to the educational committee at the business meeting, basing your stand on my deviations from Freudian theory, I would ask you to bring your official influence to bear in barring such candidates and analysts. I can do nothing in the matter because I do not share your views but continue to maintain that I am the exponent of the true and consistent therapeutic technique and theory which is in complete agreement with clinical analytic work, and I certainly do not advocate any deviations that are more dangerous than those that can be discerned in any other analyst.

Very sincerely yours,

(signed) WILHELM REICH

(Reich to publishers of I.P.A.)

Dr. Wilhelm Reich
temporarily, Vienna I
Barawitzkagasse 6
Vienna, March 17, 1933

To the
Editorial Management and Advisory Board of the
International Psychoanalytic Publishers
Vienna I

Yesterday Dr. Freud, the editorial director, advised me that, following a decision of the advisory board and the publishers, the contract for my book "Character Analysis," scheduled for early publication, has been cancelled. The decision was based on current political conditions which make it seem inappropriate to publicize my already compromised name officially. I am disregarding my rights as a registered and active member of the IPV; I can even appreciate the precautionary measures of the board and the publishers, although, as a working scholar, I cannot approve of them. Beyond this, however, I feel obligated, in the name of the psychoanalytic movement, or at least a part of it, to call attention to the illusions apparently harbored by the editors and the publishers.

1. For a long time, political reaction has identified psychoanalysis with *Kulturbolschewismus*, and rightly so. The discoveries of psychoanalysis are diametrically opposed to the nationalistic ideology and threaten its existence. It makes absolutely no difference whether the representatives of psychoanalysis resort to one precautionary measure or another, whether they withdraw from scientific work, or whether they adapt it to present conditions. The sociological and cultural-political character of psychoanalysis cannot be eliminated from this world by any measure whatsoever. The nature of its discoveries (infantile sexuality, sexual repression, sexuality and religion) makes it the arch-enemy of political reaction. One may hide behind such illusory beliefs as a "nonpolitical" science: this will only harm scientific research, but will never prevent the ruling powers from sensing the dangers where indeed they are, and fighting them accordingly. (For example, the burning of Freud's books.)

2. Since psychoanalysis, in the unanimous opinion of its exponents, has a cultural and political significance beyond its medical goals and will play a decisive role in the forthcoming struggle for a new social order, but will certainly not side with political reaction, any attempt at adapting or camouflaging the movement's essential meaning is a senseless self-sacrifice. All the more so as a substantial group of analysts is determined to continue the cultural-political struggle. The existence of this group, regardless of its position inside or outside the IPV, is politically compromising even if its principal spokesmen should be physically de-

stroyed. I see no possibility for the leaders of the IPV to disavow this group since it is rooted completely, and in contradistinction to other groups, in the soil of psychoanalytic discoveries with all their implications.

3. No matter how difficult and complicated the relationship between psychoanalysis and the revolutionary workers' movement; no matter how uncertain the final outcome of the conflict between psychoanalysis and Marxism—no one can shake the objective truth that analytic theory is revolutionary and therefore committed to the workers' movement, independently of individual member attitudes. Therefore, I feel that today's most important task is not to secure the existence of the analysts at any price, but the continued development of psychoanalysis itself. This first of all calls for discarding any illusions and for realizing that the so-called treasures of culture have only *one* administrator: the working class and its allied intelligentsia which is now paying a heavy price in blood in the German Reich. Hitler's rule does not spell the end of the historical process. If ever the historical *raison d'être* of psychoanalysis and its sociological function was needed, the current phase of historical development must prove it.

> Very truly yours,
> (signed) WILHELM REICH

(*Reich to Anna Freud*)

April 11, 1933

My dear Miss Freud:

Yesterday I wrote you an official letter requesting the executive committee of the IPV to take a stand on my move to Copenhagen as a training and control analyst. Now you may be surprised to receive a personal letter on the same subject. But since the personal intrigues of some colleagues have gone beyond certain limits and impede any objective settlement of the matter, I am taking the liberty of turning to you, particularly as I do not know at this moment how to counter these machinations.

When they learned that I was going to Copenhagen, two Danish students wanted to study with me. They discussed this with several Viennese analysts. One of these analysts discouraged them because a training course with me allegedly would not be recognized. This man knew more than I did. Another promised the bewildered Danes to consult local training analysysts, and came back with the information that a training analysis with me was not advisable because the Danes were Marxists, and since I, too, was a Marxist, "the danger of identification" would be "too great." This came as quite a surprise to me, for up to now it seemed virtually taken for granted that theologians were sent to Pfister, moral philosophers to Mueller-Braunschweig, and reconstructed socialists to Bernfeld. Only in my case this *Gleichschaltung*,[6] to use the latest [Nazi] term, does not seem to apply. I am powerless against such methods, which I hesitate to describe more succinctly; neither do I fear them. So far I have always tried to ignore them, preferring to get to work and settling any pending conflicts in a reasonable spirit through official channels. Since I do not want to resort to the same methods at any price nor provoke a scandal, I must have an even greater concern for the official stand of the IPV, so that every-

[6] *Gleichschaltung* means the political alignment of individuals and organizations with the Hitler regime. Reich uses the term to indicate that analysts and analysands used to be paired off in accordance with similarity of background.

one, including my "sympathizers," will know what is what. In your capacity as secretary of the IPV, you are qualified, as well as undoubtedly interested, in clarifying matters, if only because this scandalous situation cannot be kept secret for long. While I can keep quiet, I cannot prevent the Danes from spreading the news all around. I can only assure you that this affair will cause quite a commotion in Denmark and Sweden.

I again appeal to you personally to intervene and speed up the official response. I have to know whether or not the analyses conducted by myself and my friends in Copenhagen will be recognized by the IPV. Since a number of Berlin analysts will probably also settle in the North, I am responsible not only to them but also to those who will study with us.

I do not know if you realize that Dr. Harnik is going to Copenhagen as a training analyst, with the explicit consent of Dr. Eitingon. Dr. Harnik's psychotic illness makes such a move seem extremely questionable. I refrain from describing the serious complications that are bound to arise when his psychosis breaks out in the North. It obviously will not help the cause of analysis. In any event, Dr. Eitingon bears a heavy responsibility for placing Dr. Harnik in such an exposed position.

Respectfully yours,

(signed) WILHELM REICH

(*Reich to Federn*)

Vienna, April 18, 1933

My dear Doctor:

About six days ago, in your capacity as acting chairman of the Psychoanalytic Association and in the name of several colleagues, you demanded that I give up public lectures in socialist and communist working-class circles. You based this request on the prevailing political climate and on the danger which threatens psychoanalysis from political reaction. At that time I told you that I could not give you such an explicit promise but that, if I received a lecture invitation from any organization, I would be ready to get in touch with you before I accepted; furthermore, I said that I planned to stay in Vienna only for another ten or fourteen days and that the probability of my speaking in public during that time was negligible. I also pointed out that the avoidance of public talks, for the reasons you stated, could only foster an illusion since the previous publications and the previous work—and especially the nature of psychoanalysis itself—can never be argued away when faced by political reaction. On April 16th, you informed me on the telephone that my explanations and my promise to communicate with you in each separate case were not sufficient, but that you had to insist on my guarantee not to give lectures. I requested a written confirmation, whereupon you informed me that you were acting in behalf of Prof. Freud. I repeated that I could not make this kind of commitment, whereupon you barred me from participating in the meetings of the Association. On April 17, 1933, I received the following letter from you: "In accordance with your wishes, I herewith repeat my earlier verbal request in writing, namely, to refrain from lecturing or debating in political meetings—particularly communist ones—here in Austria. Since the Executive Committee cannot meet at the present time, I have taken this step on my own responsibility. You are free to appeal to the Committee. I request confirmation in writing. . . ." I also note that you told my wife on the telephone that, if you were in my position, you would have resigned from the Psychoanalytic Association long ago.

Let me assure you, my dear Doctor, that I am at least as concerned about the fate of the psychoanalytic movement as you are, although I started out from a different premise and have reached a different stand. At this time, without wishing to go into the basic question of my membership, I would like to observe, however, that the basic principles involved here force me to regard the steps you have taken up to now as *private* measures —a view to which I am fully entitled by virtue of the formal aspects of this matter. If my assurances do not satisfy you, it is within your province to bring about a decision of the entire executive committee or, for that matter, of the plenum; without such a decision I cannot feel in any way committed, and even then I would have to reserve the right for the final word about carrying on my work, which, as you should know, is not strictly political but deals with the theoretical and practical application of psychoanalysis in the field of sociology. I fully appreciate the difficult position in which the official representatives of psychoanalysis find themselves now with regard to my person, but I am unable to do anything about it, because it is not rooted in my person but in the very nature of psychoanalytic research and activity. As a member of the IPV, permit me to repeat in writing that we should try to find a solution in common discussion. However, I must reject the manner in which you have tried to solve the problem as being fruitless and merely complicating the issue.

Yours very truly,

(signed) WILHELM REICH

(Reich to Anna Freud)
To the
Secretariat of the IPV

Vienna, April 22, 1933

My dear Miss Freud:

In order to avoid misunderstandings, I wish to go over the state of affairs in yesterday's board meeting of the Vienna Psychoanalytic Association. In view of the current political situation, the board of the Association asked me to stop my political work and my sociological-scientific publications. It demanded an explicit promise, although I explained that circumstances would not permit me anyway to continue with this work as I had done before, thus meeting the wishes of the board halfway. I declared that I could not give such a promise. However, I did propose that I would suspend further publications for a year or two, on *one* condition: provided the IPV took an official stand on my work, to create a basis for deciding whether my work and my theory of sex-economy could be reconciled with my membership or not. I have the greatest interest in eliminating two facts: first, the IPV's strategy of "killing by silence" as hitherto applied to my work, and, secondly, the resultant attempts to give me the cold shoulder unofficially, quietly, as it were by indirection. Dr. Eitingon's private stand on the question of my call to Copenhagen as a training analyst, of which I informed you; Dr. Federn's private proposal that I should be induced to resign from the IPV; the private attempts by several analysts to dispute my competence to train analysts and to disavow my purely analytic work—these represent inappropriate attempts to resolve a conflict which can only be clarified by an open, official stand. Yesterday I tried to show where the difficulty lies: the various official functionaries of the IPV who are against me are hard put to prove that I have ceased to be a legitimate exponent of psychoanalysis and that my theories are outside the admissible scope of variations. On the other hand, the nature of my work has become uncomfortable. Although I fully understand the resultant tendency, namely, to resolve this without fuss, in the interest of this historically significant conflict within the psychonanalytic movement I cannot absolve the IPV from taking an official stand. I therefore declared last night that under no circumstances would I voluntarily resign from the IPV, no matter how great the humiliations and unofficial acts of injustice; not the least of my reasons is that I regard myself as one of the few truly legitimate exponents of psychoanalysis and am regarded as such by an important number of IPV members. Upon mature consideration, I find that there is no other solution except this: either the IPV will dissociate itself, factually and organizationally, from my concept that psychoanalysis is a basic element of *Kulturbolschewismus*[7] and is combated as such by the political reaction, or else it will grant me the same freedom of research and work within the framework of the IPV that is granted, as a matter of course, to other trends.

You will surely understand that before making any further decisions, I will have to await the IPV's stand on Dr. Eitingon's opinion, to the effect that not only my sociological but also my purely clinical-analytic teaching activity in Copenhagen should be prohibited.

Looking forward to an early reply from the secretariat, I am,

Very sincerely yours,

(signed) WILHELM REICH

[7] "The term 'Kulturbolschewismus' has, in this context, nothing whatsoever to do with the Communist Party. It was a term used by Hitler to denounce any kind of progressive or liberal thinking, especially in the realm of mental hygiene and infant upbringing." Note added by Reich in 1952.

(*Reich to Rado*)

Webers Hotel
Copenhagen, May 1, 1933

Dr. S. Rado
New York

Dear Dr. Rado:

You may be surprised to hear from me after such a long silence. However, I feel you're among the few colleagues with good judgment, and since the present situation is so confused and difficult that one has to keep a clear head to master it, I would like to have your opinion. To get to the point: as you can well imagine, I had to leave Berlin, giving up practically all laboriously achieved previous positions, prospects, and hopes, to say nothing of material losses. Collapse on all fronts, disappointments in former bulwarks, as well as serious personal troubles, were unable to shatter my optimism, but man does not live by optimism alone. Right now I'm sitting here in Copenhagen (because in Austria there will soon be the same conditions as in Germany), and I even have excellent possibilities for earning my living, better than elsewhere. But, wild as I am, I'm determined to get back into an atmosphere where I can be not just a well-behaved analyst and "leader" of a new psychoanalytic group, but where I can continue with the sociological and cultural-political aspects of my work. For this, Copenhagen is too narrow, remote and small. I plan to stay here for about a year, but would like to start looking around to see if I might go to America. Naturally, here, too, I would have to make a living as a psychoanalyst. Considering the prevailing conflicts, the question is whether or not the New York group would allow me to stay alive. Please don't diagnose paranoia! Actually, some shocking things have happened, and you're familiar with some. I have the misfortune to be an extremely orthodox analyst and a Marxist all in one, which in our present world has produced some very unpleasant truths. Therefore Eitingon has decreed that I have no right to train analysts in Copenhagen. (Harnik, however, has been officially authorized, which is a calamity for psychoanalysis in Scandinavia.) Sweden declares that I cannot go there under any circumstances because I am a Communist. Federn has requested my resignation from the IPV. Anna Freud had a third party ask me to stop my publications and lectures. I could not make such a promise, but even assuring her that conditions per se would hinder me for some time to come was not satisfactory enough.

Hence, could you investigate and let me know how the Americans feel about me? And if I could eventually get a purely formal invitation from overseas for visa purposes?

I would also be grateful if, in your capacity as secretary of the IUK of the IPV, you would take a stand on my teaching activity in Copenhagen by writing officially to Berlin to the Educational Committee. The passage from Eitingon's letter reads:

"I was interested in reading what you write about yourself and your plans, and must state the following: from the attitude of the overwhelming majority of the Educational Committee members of the German Psychoanalytic Association toward you, it should be obvious that we cannot authorize you to teach. (The truth is that the majority of the members are *for* me. W.R.) Also, in my capacity as chairman of the IUK, I must call your explicit attention to the fact that the persons you have called upon to establish a psychoanalytic institute are doing so at their own risk and must realize that the recognition of such an institute by the IPV might encounter difficulties."

That's clear enough!

How are you and your wife?

With kindest regards to you and your family,

> Yours,
>
> (signed) WILHELM REICH

(*Eitingon to Reich*)

GERMAN PSYCHOANALYTIC ASSOCIATION

Berlin, May 19, 1933

My dear Colleague:

In reply to your letter to the educational committee of our Psychoanalytic Association, I wish to inform you of the following:

In general, applications of candidates for membership in our Association are recognized provided the training analyses have been conducted by older members of the Association and the judgment of the training analyst agrees with that of the control analyst—both functions cannot be held by the same person—and provided the plenary session of the Association, following the candidate's lecture, has become convinced of his qualifications.

In cases like yours, where there are differences between an older member and the educational committee of the Association about scientific-theoretical and practical-technical problems of psychoanalysis, there is of course a stronger emphasis on the opinion of the control analyst and the plenary session of the Association in considering admission to membership.

> Yours truly,
>
> (signed) M. EITINGON

(*Reich to the German Psychoanalytic Association*)

Copenhagen, May 30, 1933

To the Executive Committee of the
German Psychoanalytic Association
Berlin

Dr. Eitingon's letter of May 19th, written in the name of the German Psychoanalytic Association, not only contained information that surprised me but also confused a situation which, in the interests of all concerned, would require the earliest possible clarification. First of all, it is asserted that there are scientific and technical differences between me and the Executive Committee. Surely such differences would have become apparent in the many lectures and seminars I have given over the years under the auspices of the Association. I was convinced of the contrary because several members of the Educational Committee—such as Dr. Simmel, Dr. Boehm, Dr. Fenichel, Dr. Mueller-Braunschweig—repeatedly declared that my theoretical and technical concepts were completely in line with legitimate psychoanalysis. Only Dr. Eitingon argued against me, whereupon, as the minutes must show, his criticism was refuted by several speakers during the discussion. Therefore I find it incomprehensible how such an assertion as the one mentioned above ever could have been made. For this reason I very much hope that the Executive Committee of the group I belong to will take the occasion of my forthcoming book, "Character Analysis," [1] either to dissociate itself from my work or to confirm its basic analytic validity. Surely you will understand that I cannot permit differences in philosophical outlook to be shifted to another field and that I would like to claim the same rights with regard to philosoph-

[1] Published independently in 1933.

ical concepts that are unreservedly granted to other colleagues.

As to the factual side of my pedagogic authority, I wish to remind you that for more than a decade I have conducted training and control analyses; furthermore, for six years, as head of the Vienna technical seminar, I have held the same concepts that I hold today, and yet the question of limiting my authority to teach never came up. The remedy for this situation as proposed in the letter of the Executive Committee—namely, to submit my students to stricter control—signifies in effect not only a vote of no confidence and a curtailment of my work as an analyst: it is also otherwise highly arguable. Up to now I have taken it for granted that I would control and judge any candidates analyzed by my colleagues not as a matter of form or out of regard for the person of the analyst but solely on the basis of their ability. I have always expected the same from any colleagues who would carry on the further training of my analysands. Your letter, however, clearly shows that my natural assumption was an illusion and that personal, and not factual, considerations decide the issue. As a training analyst, I was fully conversant with the basic tenets of the bylaws, and their repetition failed to answer the question I posed in my letter to the Executive Committee. . . .

As a member of the German Psychoanalytic Association, I would request the Executive Committee to explain the scientific and technical differences it has hinted at (my own concepts can always be checked in my publications) and then come to a clearcut decision. I wish to assure you that I do not want to cause unnecessary difficulties; on the contrary, I wish to help eliminate those that now exist; furthermore, I am prepared to settle all questions in a friendly way and with the necessary analytic frankness. However, because I have no talent for it, I am incapable of responding in kind to tactics designed to obscure the facts—tactics which, judging by all that has transpired up to now, are apparently aimed at *cold-shouldering* me.

Very truly yours,
(signed) WILHELM REICH

(*Erik Carstens to Freud*)

10 November 1933

DANISH PSYCHOANALYTIC ASSOCIATION
Holbersgade 26 — Copenhagen K

My dear Professor:

The Danish Psychoanalytic Association has asked me to write you as follows:

We are turning to you, the founder of psychoanalytic science, to help us in our difficulties.

Our efforts in behalf of psychoanalysis are threatened from two sides—by the Danish authorities and the "wild" analysts.

Without motivation, our Minister of Justice has rejected our petition for residence and working permit for Dr. Reich, who is our training analyst and scientific director. We replied by inviting the public to a lecture, where Reich, Neergaard and I discussed the "Struggle for Psychoanalysis." The evening was a success, about 600 people attended, the press gave us good coverage, and a group of physicians decided to send a new petition to the Minister of Justice. We have written to Dr. E. Jones, asking him for his expert opinion on the need of authorized training for psychoanalysts, for submission to the Danish authorities.

The next attack on psychoanalysis happened a few days ago:

the Attorney General is suing the editor of a journal for publishing an article by Dr. Reich on sexual education which he considers pornographic. This article is a translation of Reich's paper published in 1928 in the *Journal for Psychoanalytic Pedagogy*.[2]

We are determined to continue the struggle for authorized psychoanalytic training, but are further handicapped by the activities of wild analysts. One of them, Sigurd Naesgaard, Ph.D., who has never been analyzed, has battled for years against the training analysis. He asserts that the training analysis is only a means of power. Publicly, he describes himself as your student, but his publications contain such a mixture of opinions by Stekel, Adler, Jung and yourself that no one can quite unravel who said what. He has asked many persons to practice psychoanalysis without previous training. Several have followed his suggestion. Recently he founded, together with Strömme (Oslo) and Bjerre (Stockholm) a Scandinavian Psychotherapeutic Association for the purpose of establishing psychotherapeutic training institutes. In the program brochure, the training analysis is not even mentioned.

I am writing in such detail about Dr. Naesgaard because I know that you have corresponded with him and because I must assume that, living as far away as you do, you are not fully informed about him. A friend of mine who knows Naesgaard quite well recently told me that Naesgaard showed him a letter from you, in which you mentioned Harnik and Reich. You apparently wrote about Harnik that you had known for years that he was manic-paranoid. As to your comment on Reich, my friend had promised to keep silent.

[2] "Wohin fuehrt die Nackterziehung." Included in *The Sexual Revolution*, p. 61.

You will scarcely be able to judge from such a distance how much Harnik has damaged the psychoanalytic movement here. My letter would be very long indeed if I were to elaborate on this. Let me just say this: people in Copenhagen were greatly surprised, and still are, that a man in his condition was a member of the teaching committee of the German Psychoanalytic Association, that he was given the difficult assignment to teach psychoanalysis in Denmark, and that he was an authorized analyst at all.

In contrast to Harnik, Dr. Reich has rendered us such valuable practical assistance as a training analyst and director of our technical seminar during his brief residence that we wish to keep him at all costs. His departure would not only disrupt our training program but would also cause great personal harm since our training analyses would suddenly stop. Most of us are prevented by external circumstances from following him abroad. But for several analysands with strong transference feelings such a break would be just as harmful as an interrupted operation would be for a patient whose doctor leaves him in the middle of surgery.

Therefore, we would appreciate your helping us in this trying situation by sending us your expert opinion on these two questions:

1) Is a training analysis mandatory for those who wish to practice psychoanalysis?

2) Is Reich's article "Where Does Nudist Education Lead To?" (Journal for ps. Pedagogy, 1928) pornographic?

We further would ask your permission to forward your opinions to the Danish authorities and also—if we consider it appropriate, to publish them in Denmark. Please allow us to observe that we are in urgent need of this testimony and shall be most grateful to have it.

Very respectfully yours,
(signed) ERIK CARSTENS

[Freud's reply, dated November 12, 1933, acknowledged Reich's stature as an analyst, but criticized his political ideology, which he felt interfered with his scientific work. Carsten's appeal for help was rejected.]

(*Reich to Fenichel*)

Malmo, March 26, 1934

To Otto Fenichel
For Dissemination to
All Analysts in Sympathy with Marxism
Oslo

Dear Colleagues:

Otto Fenichel's report on conditions in the IPV is extremely disturbing to every psychoanalyst who is deeply concerned with psychoanalytic research, but to me it does not present anything substantially new. I feel that the catastrophic conditions prevailing in the whole world have merely brought to a head long-standing conditions within the psychoanalytic movement itself —partly driven to the surface and visible to all, and partly sharpened to the point of absurdity, as in the political switch-over of German psychoanalysts who prior to Hitler's seizure of power were regarded as completely reliable. The ideological struggle within psychoanalysis—science and Marxism[3] versus mysticism

---

[3] The term "Marxist" or "dialectical materialistic" is used in agreement with the view, then prevalent, that they meant "scientific" and "rational" in contradistinction to metaphysics, which was considered bourgeois.

and reaction—has been forming for a long time, having been fought partly underground and partly in opposition to my own psychoanalytic and sociological work as far back as 1925. It is currently forcing a crisis in psychoanalytic research and the whole psychoanalytic movement which can, and will be, jointly determined by us and will press for a solution at the next Congress. Hence those who want to serve the cause should obtain complete clarity about the background of the conflict, its current structure and the probabilities of its future course.

I wish to inform you that I am now preparing a presentation of the basic differences of opinion, together with their histories and consequences, which I shall be glad to submit for discussion as soon as I have completed it. This letter is not intended to clarify the problems but merely to point up those issues which, in my opinion, will have to be placed in the foreground in the near future if we are to proceed correctly. Fenichel has done us a great service with his comprehensive report. But beyond this, the situation requires clarification on the following points:

1. In science, a political struggle usually does not present itself directly and thus is not easily recognizable, but is camouflaged as a difference of scientific theories. It requires considerable Marxist training to recognize whether such differences merely stem from factual confusion or whether, regardless of the facts, they arise from conflicting political ideologies. I do not consider it very promising to wage a struggle within a scientific movement with weapons taken from the arsenal of party politics. I mean, it is not important to prove that one school of thought is reactionary and the other revolutionary. What matters is not so much the private political conviction of the analyst; rather, it is important to show how the ideology of a scholar will influence the formation of his theory and his clinical, therapeutic

work. Any critique of psychoanalysis must grow from the subject matter itself; it must demonstrate from the raw material of research in which particular concepts the road forks off—to the right, or to the left. Therefore, dialectical-materialist criticism of the psychoanalytic movement can only be fruitful if it proceeds from a specific standpoint it has already earned independently —in other words, from a theory. A concrete example: it is certainly characteristic that the attitude of the Paris group toward the German émigrés was reactionary. But what is decisive for the development of psychoanalysis is the fact not only that today Laforgue's[4] theories are published in preference to authentic psychoanalytic works but that this distortion of psychoanalysis goes unopposed, even among analysts who have been the most dependable in the past. Therefore, whoever does not take an open stand against the wrong theories we criticize supports them, whether he likes to or not, and runs the danger of slipping into the wrong path. For my part, since 1924, when I saw the beginnings of a schism in the formation of analytic theory, I have tried to gain a firm foothold for my criticism by the consistent development of the psychoanalytic libido theory. The attacks of the most prominent members of the Vienna association (Deutsch, Federn, Nunberg, etc.) on my orgasm theory were the first signs of the conflict between dialectical-materialist and bourgeois psychoanalysis at a time when neither side was aware of it. Even then Freud seemed to realize the depth of the conflict. He once said to me after a lecture: "Either you are completely wrong, or you will soon have to carry the heavy burden of psychoanalysis alone." I knew I was not basically wrong, and today I know that the second part of Freud's prediction has

[4] René Laforgue, French psychoanalyst, author of *Clinical Aspects of Psycho-analysis.*

come true for me. So I already have my own theoretical platform on which to base my militant criticism. I suggest that you also find a theoretical position. Which brings me to the second point.

2. I think that in Fenichel's report I have lately detected a tendency that has always caused me great concern. I fully appreciate it, but for purely objective reasons I cannot agree with it. This tendency reads: "Wherever possible, Freud himself should be kept out of the conflict." And this is precisely what cannot be done. It is taken for granted that in tone and attitude our criticism of Freud will differ from our criticism of Roheim, but we cannot, and should not, exclude Freud from criticism. For we must note the following:

a. The scientific sins of Roheim,[5] Laforgue, Jones, Klein,[6] Deutsch, etc., are more or less rooted in Freud.

b. The basic debate between dialectical-materialist and bourgeois psychoanalysts will primarily have to prove where Freud the scientist came into conflict with Freud the bourgeois philosopher; where psychoanalytic research corrected the bourgeois concept of culture and where the bourgeois concept of culture hindered and confused scientific research and led it astray. "Freud against Freud" is the central theme of our criticism. Not for one moment should we put our consideration for Freud before our consideration for the future of psychoanalysis. And from my personal relationship with Freud I have come to the conclusion that he would prefer it this way, all appearances to the contrary.

3. I feel chiefly responsible for the conflict that has become so

[5] Géza Róheim (1891-1953), anthropologist who applied psychoanalysis to the study of primitive peoples, particularly in Australia.
[6] Melanie Klein (1882-1960), whose psychoanalytic studies were principally with children.

acute, for I was already in the midst of the dispute with Freud when even my best friends kept insisting that all would be well "if only I were not so aggressive." This personal comment is understandable; I do not wish to deny that my tactics were not always clever and that at one time I felt it was really important whether Deutsch was a good or a bad analyst. I first had to understand what was at stake when the analysts denied the role of genitality in the therapy of the neuroses, or the significance of negative transference, etc. It was much too late that I realized we were separated by an ideological gulf. But I must also note that even in 1930, when I moved to Berlin, my reports on the concepts of the Vienna analysts were not given credence, that my dispute with Alexander in 1927 about the need for punishment was considered exaggerated, that even today my fight against the death-instinct theory is not taken seriously enough, and that my economic concept of the neuroses is still regarded as Reich's private whim. I do not mention this because I want to boast about being right. You may be sure that I have other matters to worry about, for instance: The awareness of differences within a movement is often useless if it arrives too late; we can never work hard enough to recognize and articulate these differences, which some day may acquire great significance, and to understand the perspectives of the development. I am convinced that in the none too distant future psychoanalysis will play a powerful role in resolving the battles of our century. This will require great responsibility, lack of illusions, hard, uncompromising work, the clearest scientific perspective and the ruthless severing of all personal ties with those persons who have always given the impression that they would only stand in the way. If we do not admit our past mistakes, we will commit the same mistakes in the future—to the detriment of the cause. The present state of affairs would not have spread to such an extent if Freud had not supported the reactionary trends and combated the Marxist trends. I wish to remind you of his steps concerning my paper "The Masochistic Character" in 1931, of Fenichel's removal as editor of the *Journal* because he would not suppress the left, of his refusal of organizational support in the Copenhagen, pornography affair, of the Naesgaard letter in which Freud said (incidentally, to a wild analyst) that my ideology interfered with my scientific work, which Naesgaard circulated all over Copenhagen, and of many other big and small actions: among them Freud's complete silence on the concepts I developed about anxiety, character, technique, orgasm theory, etc., all of which have become indispensable and are tacitly accepted by many but remain officially opposed. You must understand that I have to protect my work, not because I have taken offense but because I believe that I have developed psychoanalysis along the most consistent scientific course. If people kill our work by silence—unless they just plagiarize and distort it, as Balint did at the last Congress—we must not only vigorously defend ourselves and even move to the attack, but we must have the courage of our own convictions. We must discard all false modesty and take the position that *we* are carrying on scientific—i.e., Marxist, dialectical-materialist—psychoanalysis, and that we are determined to defend it even against Freud wherever he is inconsistent. You know by and large where the development of analytic theory has taken me: to the creation of a scientific sphere for which I have suggested the name of sex-economy and political psychology. Much as I regard myself as a psychoanalyst in the truest sense, today I belong just as much to a new discipline which grew from the border realm between Marxist sociology and method on the one hand and psychoanalytic clinical work and psychology on the other. Since my path has been consistently determined for a long time to come, but since very few sympathizing analysts share my basic views, my position in the present conflict will perhaps be somewhat different. However, I believe that ways for common action can be found. My suggestions to Fenichel's questions about the future attitude of the members of the IPV are briefly the following:

1. Not only independent research, but also sharp, factual, impersonal criticism of our opponents.

2. All convinced dialectical-materialist psychoanalysts should be merged into an opposing group within the IPV. Exclusion should be neither feared nor provoked. Young analysts and potential sympathizers should be won over by specialized scientific work and irrefutable criticism. They should be grouped around the nucleus of the organization which in turn would give them scientific and organizational support.

3. Training reform and expansion. I think the following points are indispensable, although they cover by no means everything: any candidate's admission to the organization and to clinical practice should be predicated on the judgment of the training analysts about the applicant's libido economy (reason: the catastrophic influence of analysts with sex neuroses); thorough training in the correct application of psychoanalysis to sociology; knowledge of the basic elements of Marxism; sound knowledge of sexology, an indispensable prerequisite for all therapeutic activity. Clergymen and reactionary-minded physicians who in analysis fail to recognize the contradiction between sexual reality and social ideology cannot become analysts. . . .

Everything else will, and can be, settled only in the continuing intramural debate about psychoanalysis.

(signed) WILHELM REICH

(Reich to dialectical materialistic psychoanalysts)

Malmo, May 30, 1934

To the Group of
Dialectical Materialistic Psychoanalysts
Attn: Otto Fenichel
Oslo

Dear Colleagues and Comrades:

When my further residence in Sweden was turned down owing to denunciations by psychiatrists, as it recently turned out, a group of psychoanalysts and sympathizers wrote a circular letter to Freud, Einstein, Bohr and Malinowski, asking them to protest in writing against the persecution of scientists by political reactionaries. Freud declined: "In matters of Dr. W.R. I cannot join your protest." This attitude of Freud's may perhaps have serious and decisive consequences for the next psychoanalytic congress. It is therefore necessary to clarify its nature and meaning. It is, after all, consistent with Freud's position in the pornography affair in Copenhagen which resulted in a sixty-day jail sentence for the editor of the "Plan."

Freud's personal motives may be extremely interesting, but for judging the over-all situation they are immaterial. The question cannot be clarified by pointing to his age, his weariness, his private convictions, etc. What concerns us here is an essential part of the struggle between reaction and revolution. The foundation of psychoanalysis was no more a personal, private act than was the book-burning in Berlin in 1933; the same goes for the correspondence between Einstein and Freud about the war[7] and, for that matter, the refusal to judge whether an article published in an official pedagogic journal was pornographic or not.

[7] Reference to "Why War?", open letters between Einstein and Freud, published originally in the *New Commonwealth*, London, 1934.

Nor are we concerned with "unmasking" Freud, as some colleagues feel, but we are exclusively preoccupied with the political and cultural position of psychoanalysis in today's world.

Surely this question cannot be decided only theoretically, in scholarly treatises, but must be solved in practice—to the advantage of the political left—by clearly separating the factions within the IPV. Precisely how to proceed would have to be the object of detailed consultations before the Congress. The Marxist analysts must expect that the IPV, whose leadership maneuvers with great diplomatic skill, will do everything to eliminate them. I feel that we will have to make every possible preparation to increase our influence so that we can explain objectively to the Congress what goals are at stake: the preservation, security and continuance of psychoanalytic research and the movement itself. Therefore, in my opinion, Freud should not be personally blamed for his intransigence. To the contrary, his attitude is a symptom of the scientific tension within the IPV, and we must explain this tension as an expression of the fight about the cultural-political significance of psychoanalysis. This will emphasize that *we* are the exponents of Freud's basic principles, and that psychoanalysis is not merely a medical discipline but, beyond that, a doctrine of historical significance. Now is the time to prove why psychoanalysis has this significance, and why its function can be fulfilled in the camp of the political left alone. We have to prove that there is no point in abstract discussions of this cultural-political significance, as the conservative analysts do, but to turn this significance into reality, both in concrete practice and in theory.

With kindest regards,

(signed) WILHELM REICH

(Reich to analysts in opposition to Freud)

July 21, 1934 [8]

To the Group of
Analysts in Opposition
through Otto Fenichel
Oslo

I just received a letter from Otto Fenichel informing me that the discussion with the Prague analysts about the differences between Fenichel and me as revealed during the Humlebaek debate has resulted in complete agreement with Fenichel. I cannot determine whether this would have happened if I had participated in the meeting. Here Fenichel's moderating standpoint, which does *not* grasp my basic concept, was completely rejected not only by the Danish candidates but also by Gerö and Liebeck. Grave, decisive problems are at stake; they cannot be eliminated by any attempt to reconcile insurmountable contradictions, as Fenichel has tried to do, to the detriment of factual clarity. You all know my stand, my own theoretical basis, and those points of psychoanalytic theory that have brought me into conflict with Freud. To give but *one* example: Fenichel's attitude toward this conflict was already revealed at the Oslo meeting, where he declared in his lecture that since the "Three Contributions" nothing important has appeared on the theory of sexuality. He had forgotten my orgasm theory. It is now clear that this was not a meaningless lapse. He seriously maintained that the function of the orgasm had been presented by Freud long ago. I have a reason for stressing this one example among many others. Historically, all differences between the Marxist

---

[8] This letter was not sent.

and the non-Marxist concept of psychoanalysis have evolved precisely around this question. Moreover, this was the point where for the first time I discovered the moral and political bias of the analysts, where I first felt what it meant to reveal such important facts that have been neglected through unconscious intent. Even in the preface to my orgasm book,[9] when I was still far from having obtained political and sex-political clarity, I had to admit that on the basis of my experiences I could not pride myself in describing the orgasm theory as a part of generally accepted psychoanalysis. We are not concerned with priority but with facts: it turned out that Fenichel had neither emotional nor scientific understanding for the sex-economic significance of the problem. But everything hinges on the stand that is taken toward this question, for from here—*and from here alone* —can everything or nothing of what I worked out in painful struggles over the past twelve years be understood. Those who want to understand the current main conflict in psychoanalysis must first understand this. If Fenichel were right, we surely would have heard at least some comment on the orgastic function either from Nunberg's compilation or from Freud's second series of lectures. Please understand that on this point I must remain absolutely firm and cannot make any concessions whatsoever. No one will relieve me of the responsibility for everything that depends on it. When I have more time, I will sit down and work out the full picture for you.

As for the procedure at the Congress, I would once more like to define my position:

1. If it turns out that the young Berlin analysts present cor-

[9] *Die Funktion des Orgasmus* (Leipzig, Vienna, Zurich: Internationaler Psychoanalytischer Verlag, 1927).

rect psychoanalytic concepts and my clinical views, I will support the continued functioning of the Berlin association; otherwise, not.

2. For the time being I will do nothing about the political aspect of the movement at the Congress. Whether and how I act will depend on the whole opposition's attitude in looking after the interests of psychoanalytic research. Owing to the decisive theoretical differences within our group which have recently crystallized, I cannot commit myself. I have the impression that Fenichel, as he showed again in his latest paper on the pre-œdipal development of girls, is still trying to bridge the unbridgeable and to mend the broken pieces at all costs. He affirms my own concepts as well as those of others that are incompatible with mine, as, for instance, the role of phylogenesis. I do not wish to force a decision; I know that circumstances are stronger than I am, and will remain so for a long time to come. However, I must prevent my basic concepts, which brought me into conflict with Freud, from becoming prematurely diluted and from being ascribed to others who have rejected them. Above all, in view of the perspectives I have gained over the past months, I must prevent my instinct theory, my concept of anxiety, my technique, etc., from becoming obscured and blurred.

I am also *professionally* interested in seeing that my findings are linked with my name; neither do I want to be judged in the same category and on the same level with Melitta Schmideberg;[1] I want my writings to be studied at least as carefully as · those of Miss Searl or Harnik. I will definitely defend myself if my concepts and findings, for which I have fought hard since 1924 against all generally held opinions, are now taken for

[1] Melitta Schmideberg, psychoanalyst, daughter of Melanie Klein.

granted *without mention of my name* or are presented as new problems that have just come up.

Everyone has the chance to convince himself, to reject or to criticize as he pleases, but I must continue to protect my scientific and organizational independence. At present I can only uphold the interest of *my* work, knowing that in doing so I can preserve the best, the most revolutionary and the most progressive elements in psychoanalysis from sinking into the mire of current analytic research. So I cannot promise anything before the Congress starts except that I will once again ascertain how matters stand.

3. About demands at the Congress: I have already told Fenichel that the opposition group had better not call itself "Marxist." Then it would have greater freedom of action and could even support liberal slogans. I advised supporting liberal slogans but maintaining our own basic, negative stand on reactionary research, if [later] we intend to come forward as a Marxist group, for essentially we will not be able to conceal this appearance from the world. We will collaborate *better* if the opposition does not undertake any more than it can now perform—personally, structurally and scientifically. After all, any development is still possible. I am convinced that these inner difficulties would not exist if for years I had not worked quite openly and if many members of the opposition were not personal friends of mine as well, which seems to commit them more than the situation requires. My work happens to differ from most of those in the opposition, and, as I said before, I have other obligations and tasks besides psychoanalysis, which makes for a divergence in tactical and organizational attitudes. We should not conceal these divergences and then react with irritation and hostility. In

spite of all differences we should act in concert wherever possible, but otherwise we should act independently.

Very cordially,

(signed) WILHELM REICH

(Mueller-Braunschweig to Reich)

Berlin-Schmargendorf
August 1, 1934

My dear Colleague:

With the forthcoming Congress, the IPV publisher plans to put out a calendar listing the members of the Psychoanalytic Association. Circumstances seem to require the elimination of your name from the register of the German Psychoanalytic Society. I would greatly appreciate it if you would regard our request with understanding, relegating to the background any possible personal feelings in the interest of our psychoanalytic cause in Germany and expressing your agreement with this step.

As a scholar and author you are too well known to the international world of psychoanalysts for this omission to cause you the slightest harm, as it might, for example, affect a newcomer in the field. Furthermore, the whole problem will be academic once the Scandinavian group is recognized at the Congress, thus assuring your inclusion in future membership lists of this new group.

May I ask for your immediate reply.

With best regards,

Yours sincerely,

(signed) CARL MUELLER

(*Reich to Liebeck*[2])

(Oslo), Nov. 10, 1934

Dear Lotte Liebeck:

Your letter was a great pleasure. I might have many things to say, but will have to be brief because I have little time.

While my concept of masochism, in *Character Analysis*, wrests the problem from the metaphysical realm of the death instinct, it is still far from complete. Nevertheless, it can be comprehended; one merely has to dig deep down into the analyses to reach the anxiety about the "bursting" of the genitalia. I have now finished my Congress lecture, and was able to expand on the relation between masochism and orgasm. Should I eventually send a copy or galley proofs to the group, for critical comment?

With O.F. [Otto Fenichel] the situation is *very* difficult! This friendship and readiness to understand the orgasm theory, combined with a structural inability and unconscious hostility, is a complicated problem for me. I am glad that you could judge this for yourself when you were in Sletten. Edith[3] no doubt does not believe it.

You have good reason to be shaken by reading Freud: he was a wonderful man. But I was even more shattered by the subsequent break in his work. This is tragic. I am curious to know if you will discern it before it becomes openly manifest. It goes back to the earliest writings (predominance of symbolic interpretation rather than questions of dynamics-economy, genitality, etc.). But this can only be discovered ex post facto. Enjoy yourself, then, and good luck in your work.

[2] Lotte Liebeck, German psychoanalyst and student of Reich.
[3] Edith Jacobson, M.D.

Tomorrow will be the first decisive meeting with the physiologist. Am very excited.

Best regards to all the colleagues and to yourself.

(signed) WILHELM REICH

(*Liebeck to Reich*)

Berlin, November 22, 1934
W.9, Tirpitzufer 14

Dear Colleague:

. . . .

I would like to tell you briefly about the views I have so far reached during these studies.[4] I am really shaken. Particularly since I have now found the first break (you know that, for the time being, I'm reading only the purely theoretical writings, disregarding, for example, the dream altogether). So one evening I pick up a paper dated 1896 on "The Role of Sexuality in the Etiology . . ." And that same night I read "My views on this role . . ." 1906! And this is the first break! The first work being lucid, courageous, with a brilliant prediction about the tremendous significance of the path shown and of the insights for mankind in general. The suggestion that it is up to the coming century to build up further—and then, ten years later, a totally different man, even in tone! What once was courage and clarity, combined with the utmost caution and integrity of scientific thinking, is now replaced by anxious vacillation and the fear of his own courage. How many disappointments and personal blows there must have been in the intervening years! This consideration is not important for judging the work per *se*, nor does it

4 Liebeck refers to her study of Freud's work.

have a place in objective criticism. But personally I'm inclined to believe that the retreat was prepared by a good deal of therapeutic failure during this period. Objectively, I note that he can be beaten with his own weapons. Throughout his early works he disparaged the hereditary factor in favor of the accidental element—only to smuggle in through the back door the same factor he had previously thrown out! Sexual constitution organically determined! At one time he thought that hereditary damage was incurable anyway; now it is for us to tell him that ourselves! Constitutional damage—in that case we'll have to throw in the towel. But it is not so much the change of mind itself, and its consequences, but whether this change is in the right direction. And here he has convinced us too deeply and too eloquently for us to go along with him down this road. —Another word about the consequences: we have allowed ourselves to be seduced—more or less, and over varying periods of time—into thinking of our work as an interesting scientific activity, with the main emphasis on scientific findings. Therefore everything progressed along scientific lines. The longer I work myself, and the more courageously I do so, the more I become aware of the vast explosive element it contains. I have always sensed this, but have gone out of my way to avoid it for fear of drawing the ultimate conclusion. Our profession ceases to be *gemütlich* if we have to rake up the deepest primeval emotions! And this we must inevitably do, or else we will get stuck just as inevitably halfway in between, or worse! And once we do this, we can no longer doubt the truth of the etiology anchored in the traumatic experiences of childhood. I believe more and more that we lean, quite without cause, on fantasies, and seriously neglect actual experience. Important as the discovery of fantasies is, I'm equally convinced by the eloquence of the experiences that I can now develop with my patients. Catharsis should not be belittled, either; it is vastly underestimated. Of course it should not be treated as an isolated phenomenon but rather as a fertile soil for continued work. In my opinion it is better to overemphasize it than to throw it out the window. I'm now capable of clearly expressing and explaining what I have intuitively felt long ago. I deliberately take my cue from the works of 1896. From then on, the roads fork off. Here is how I see it: on the one hand, a continued development; on the other, a slow retreat. For some time both are in balance, and there are still many marvelous discoveries for us in subsequent writings, until the balance shifts more and more to the sterile side and leads to paths that deviate from the natural sciences. There is only one thing I don't understand: why haven't the others noticed this? Or am I doing them an injustice out of my limited knowledge of literature? But perhaps it is an indispensable existential lie to have this blind spot. Because it does make you feel a little creepy, just thinking how much there still remains to be done. Current life problems with all their complexities, the raging storms of an earlier past, to treat all of this simultaneously is a big order! But please don't discuss this letter with anyone; I plan to expand it into a major paper, perhaps in a year or two. But I would like to have your opinion, and I do want to thank you because without you I would have never been able to do it! The intellectual bluffing is over and done with. . . .

> With many thanks and affectionate regards,
> (signed) LOTTE LIEBECK

Please note my address, otherwise there will be much delay.

(Reich to psychoanalysts in Denmark, Norway and Germany who are in opposition to, and in conflict with, Freud)

Oslo, December 16, 1934

Dear Colleagues:

My exclusion from the IPV [5] resulted from a chain of circumstances that served the interests of my opponents. The German association did not actually want to exclude me and had taken it for granted that I would automatically become a member of the Scandinavian group. I was asked by numerous colleagues from various local groups to rejoin via the Norwegian group, and three members of this group, who were attending the Congress, assured me of acceptance. I could not make up my mind at that time and wished to consider the matter. Here are the names of several prominent colleagues who regarded the whole affair as a pure formality: Zulliger, Loewenstein, Bally, Landauer, Meng, Schjelderup, Hoel, Raknes, etc. When I moved to Oslo to carry out certain experiments concerning my sexual theory, people collaborated with me as if I were a member. The close connection of my work with the IPV group, and renewed assurances from colleagues in Oslo, prompted me to reapply for membership. No one had expected that Dr. Fenichel would sharply oppose me and use his influence against me. A few days earlier, I had asked Fenichel for his opinion, but he merely shrugged. The reason for his opposition is as follows: he said I harmed the cause of natural scientific (dialectical-materialist) psychoanalysis; it would be better if I remained outside and if the cause were even dissociated from my name and person.

1. *Chairman Prof. Schjelderup's stand:*

Schjelderup personally favors my readmission and only wished

[5] See Documentary Supplement, p. 255.

to bring up two questions for discussion: (a) Are we factually (orgasm theory and character analysis) in agreement with Reich? (His other activities do not concern us at all.) (b) Are we willing to take the risk connected with Reich's admission, as, for instance, exclusion of the whole group? Now Fenichel did not merely confine himself to that particular evening to state his opinion but had carried on active agitation against Reich among the members—most of whom are in analysis with him—fully aware that they were for R.

2. *Fenichel's function:*

I must recall briefly that, before I moved to Berlin, in November 1930, Fenichel had neither called himself a dialectical-materialist analyst nor was he connected with the cause in any way except through my writings which he had reviewed since 1930. In Berlin, there was soon formed a small circle of analysts who were interested in my scientific concepts, among them Fenichel. Since the situation in the association soon became difficult and the confusion in the field of libido theory—death-instinct theory was very great, and since I had no time myself, I asked Fenichel to keep the interested colleagues continually informed on the progress of the problem. I soon had the uncomfortable feeling that, although Fenichel reported on my concepts very ably and at first openly championed them, he increasingly—in direct ratio to the growing difficulties—tried to bridge contradictions, to water down concepts—in short, to reconcile all sides. In my paper "Dialectical Materialism and Psychoanalysis" I had clearly shown which of the scientific views I had always advocated were held in common. But the contradiction between the death-instinct theory and the orgasm theory, between the biologistic and the sociological concept of sexual repression, between the bourgeois-metaphysical and the dialectical-materialist ideology had to be worked out with equal clarity. I know from experience that there is no better way to serve Freud and psychoanalysis than to separate the scientific from the non-scientific within the doctrine of psychoanalysis. This is the right way to gain adherents to psychoanalysis in those circles that matter. Fenichel never wanted to commit himself unequivocally to my scientific platform. He did not want to be just one of the "Reich group," but neither did he do anything on his own to oppose the death-instinct theory and everything connected with it. Instead, he based the struggle on purely organizational questions and carried on a childish, play-acting kind of opposition. I was always against it and tried to make it clear to him that a struggle within a scientific organization must be conducted along factual and professional lines, excluding political and even organizational factors. I told him, if we arouse the professional interest of the colleagues they will be more likely to commit themselves politically and organizationally. At the Congress, colleagues who were friends of Fenichel's and had no connection with me made the same criticism (see circular letter on the Congress), and when the board resorted to all its diplomatic wiles, Fenichel caved in completely. The true reason is that he never intended to risk exclusion at all. However, he should have come out and said so, instead of hiding behind the excuse that first of all one had to have greater influence. How? By avoiding all controversy, by soft-pedaling one's own work and by alienating all sympathies by such timorous attitudes? Look how differently the non-Marxist Schjelderup stood up, purely by instinct! And look how much sympathy the Norwegians gained from his stand! Although I suffered an organizational defeat at the Congress, sympathy for me had never run so high. It was Fenichel's job to use this as the basis for his own work. Instead, because he felt I was becoming more and more of a burden, he turned against me, became vindictive and finally, as I have said, opposed my readmission—always on the pretext that he was protecting the "cause" against me.

3. I would ask you to note that I deeply regret ever having placed any confidence in Fenichel and asking for his help. I cannot entrust the dialectical-materialist theory of psychoanalysis which I have worked out over many years amidst the gravest trials to anyone else, nor can I dissociate myself from it. I have no quarrel with anyone doing exactly as he pleases, but I must defend myself against usurpers and so-called services of friendship. The concern for the "cause" of "dialectical-materialist psychoanalysis" and its core, the orgasm theory, must still be reserved for me alone. Naturally, one may hold different opinions on what I have called dialectical-materialist psychoanalysis and sex-economy. But when I describe my orgasm theory as its prime criterion and when Fenichel, as has been shown, would not accept it or misunderstood it, we are back to the unhappy confusion of terminologies and concepts. I, therefore, find myself faced with the unpleasant task of summarizing my scientific position. Basically, it contains three main parts:

1. *The concepts held in common with Freudian theory* (the materialistic dialectic already developed by Freud).

2. *Orgasm theory* and *character analysis* as consistent extensions of Freud's natural science and, simultaneously, representing those theories that I opposed to the death-instinct theory and the interpretive technique. Point 2 is still in the realm of psychoanalysis.

3. My own concepts of sexuality, based on the orgasm theory and transcending the sphere of psychology (sex-economy and sex-politics). Part 3 has merely points of contact with psycho-

analysis. It forms an independent field: the basic law of the sexual process.

Whoever expounds a "dialectical-materialist psychology" without explicitly expounding its very core, with the risks and sacrifices this entails, has simply made up his "own" dialectical-materialist psychology and is at liberty to teach it. There is nothing we can do about the nuisance of naming certain activities by whim. Even Stroemme, for example, calls himself a "psychoanalyst."

I realize that these comments on the nature and peculiarity of the scientific trend I represent will continue to be misunderstood by those who have not experienced the development of the last twelve years as I have. I can only ask you to have patience until the planned comprehensive presentation is available. The basic principles which I developed individually for special fields are set down in my published writings.

The fact that I dissociate myself from imprecise, nebulous concepts should not be held against me any more than I hold it against anyone for reacting cautiously or negatively toward my own concepts. It was from my teacher Freud that I learned the art of waiting and keeping my ideas free from undesirable interpretations and mongrelizations. I prefer to have fewer relationships and, instead, more tidiness in my work.

I would not like for this letter to be misconstrued in the sense that I am trying to alienate Fenichel's "circle" and his friends. Every colleague is of course free to identify himself with Fenichel's brand of dialectical-materialist psychoanalysis and to declare himself against my concept. But my own task is this: to continue developing the trend I have established, and to keep those groups that are interested continually informed on the progress of the work. I am also grateful for every suggestion and constructive criticism.

Finally, a few comments on the struggle for the natural scientific trend in psychoanalysis. I do not believe that this struggle can be won without a clear-cut, courageous and factual differentiation of common features and differences. Whoever fears exclusion—which is not so reprehensible—cannot take part in this struggle and is much more valuable as a quiet sympathetic bystander than he would be as an active fighter. However, it is self-evident that the victory of the scientific over the metaphysical trend in psychoanalysis will be more easily attained and secured if we succeed in revealing the various consequences inherent in the raw material of their own problems to the colleagues of all those groups that have plainly demonstrated their scientific orientation in their own work. The commitment to the dialectical-materialist trend in psychoanalysis in no way entails a similar commitment to the political trend of communism. There is no doubt that the person who is a valid scientist in his chosen professional specialty is to that extent secured against the influences of political reaction. And scientific integrity carries infinitely more weight than a political commitment. These are the natural scientists who some day will become the decisive force of social progress. They should merely recognize the sources of error in their work.

With very best regards

(signed) WILHELM REICH

(P.S. on Fenichel) [6]

(12/16/34)

Postscript

Fenichel finds himself in a grave conflict. On the one hand, he cannot deny the validity of my scientific position. On the other hand, he fears nothing more than taking an unequivocal stand for me and against Freud whenever the differences are manifest. He cannot oppose me factually without losing sympathies, and so he calls himself a friend of the cause while doing everything he can to avoid a conflict that is unavoidable anyway. No one is forced to go to battle for the natural scientific trend. Gerö declared that he is on my side, but does not want to fight for it. This is the proper attitude: Gerö will never become dishonest as long as he admits this to himself. Lantos told me that she sympathized with me, but that it was not her business and that she did not want to take any risks for it. We are on very good terms. Fenichel's attitude is insincere because he is caught in a conflict between willingness and ability. I shall no longer argue with Fenichel, but the nature of his dishonesty should be clearly set down here. Perhaps my readmission would lead to a premature exclusion of the group. In Fenichel's place, as the friend of a cause which was after all my own creation and which remains irrevocably tied to me, I would have talked with Reich, consulted him as to what could be done in order to build up enough strength for some future date; I would have named all those who might sooner or later be won over to the libido-theoretical point of view; I would have sent Reich's papers around for discussion, etc., etc. What did Fenichel do? He never unequivocally argued against the death-instinct theory; he did not dare to engage in open polemics against Freud when necessary; he pre-

[6] This postscript was not sent.

sents a theory of dialectical-materialist psychology which in its least important aspects agrees with the theory he ostensibly sympathizes with; no one knows how much scientific knowledge there really is that argues against the death-instinct theory, totem and taboo, etc.; in short, he is afraid. He might be valuable as a quiet co-worker, but he is completely unsuited to lead any scientific opposition because he is not willing to accept the slightest responsibilities.

Furthermore, he bases his position on the fact that I declared at the Congress that, from the point of view of the death-instinct theory, my exclusion was understandable, and he twists that statement to mean that I supposedly approved of my own exclusion because I had moved so far beyond psychoanalysis. However, all I said was "from the psychoanalysis of today," and I emphasized that I regard myself as the most consistent exponent of natural scientific psychoanalysis and its logical development: the exclusion was understandable but not affirmable. By his attitude, Fenichel merely upholds my opponents, instead of saying: "Reich represents scientific psychoanalysis; I, too, am opposed to the death-instinct theory. His exclusion is understandable from the viewpoint of the death-instinct theory, but from the viewpoint of natural scientific psychoanalysis it is an arbitrary decision." However, Fenichel is both terribly frightened and terribly ambitious. What he did was the inevitable result of this emotional confusion. I have neither time nor inclination for such organizational struggles. They are sterile. I have developed a specific theory, and whoever wants to can join me . . .

[end fragment]

Dear Colleague:

I'm not at all angry about your honest and friendly advice, and I'm sorry that you, too, think I'm a grouchy, growling old hermit. In many respects you're quite right, for instance, when you criticize my disposition to be hurt by unfriendly tactical or diplomatic maneuvers, instead of being armored against them. But if I were to armor myself completely, I would lose a number of good qualities. Now about my isolation: it isn't as bad as all that. Even outside the IPV there are many interested circles, which I can gauge by the general rise in interest. You're basically right, but you don't distinguish sharply enough between those who take the development seriously and those who are completely incapable of development and are just afraid without admitting it. Furthermore, in your attitude I miss an awareness that the controversy you've brought up is only an infinitesimal part of my work, and that up to now no one has shown himself to be letter-perfect in handling all these complications and difficulties. I grant you I should be "above" these things, but I wouldn't want to exchange polemics for dry-as-dust factuality. I find it hard to separate the factual from the personal, because the one acts on the other, and vice versa. . . . And I most sincerely believe that this isolation—not from Eitingon but from life itself, from the world, from all vital things and processes— will soon prove true for my opponents and hesitating "friends." This of course depends on more general problems to which I subordinate such questions as penis envy in women, etc. I find that psychoanalysis has become isolated from reality, but I have reality on my side and am not alone. I have a number of very gifted students and I could well take the line that it is nonsense to go begging: I'm the one who has something to give and those who want it should come to me. I can wait. For years I've pleaded for understanding; now I've had it. Today my influence permits me to withdraw into strictly scientific work and to break off any further debate. Neither can I waste time on diplomatic and tactical skirmishes. It's not in my nature. As I said in my letter, the best thing I can do for the cause is just to send out my publications. Our teacher spent fifteen years in isolation. I'm not striving to emulate him, but if necessary I, too, can take it. But I don't believe it will come to that, because there's too much momentum in my work. You'll be glad to hear that I'm going to hold a continuous clinical course and a technical seminar at the university; there is great interest.

. . . .

The question of the physiological measuring apparatus* will finally be settled in the next few days. Then I will begin.

I'm fine. I work a great deal, almost too much. I have many connections and people trust me. Some splendid successes in the past few months have confirmed the validity of my "line." It won't be my fault if in the course of time fewer and fewer people will want to travel by a 1915 type train when a more modern one is available.

How is the work you recently wrote me about? Have you had good results with the characterological work? I'm constantly learning, and am just beginning to understand the relation between masochism and libido stasis. This, too, encourages me not to fear isolation. I'm firmly convinced that under critical circumstances ignorance, fraud and cowardice can hold out for a

---

* Reference to equipment for the bio-electric experiments. See *The Function of the Orgasm*, Ch. IX, pp. 326-337.

while; they may even be "victorious." But the end will be all the more dark and tragic. So, dear Lotte, don't get all entangled, but remember that even the worst will eventually pass to make room for something better.

When you come here, I'll be glad to talk with you about "tactics" and "personal considerations," and if you're in the mood I'll tell you more about my many errors and weaknesses than you've imagined.

I've only scanned Kaiser's[7] paper. I was amused to see that *Imago* simultaneously published another article completely contradicting it. I've gradually learned to take this kind of thing from the humorous side, although I feel that a certain type of humor is an evasion. I believe Kaiser handled the subject too academically; he wanted to be too consistent and he went ahead too fast. He forgets that a theoretical postulate can be substantially correct but may not be easily carried into practice. His conclusion that all interpretation is superfluous is correct, but in our clinical practice we still cannot do without terminal interpretations. From my own development I disliked the academic tone: it didn't touch the essentials. But still, I liked the article. But I have one suspicion: just as they've tried to dissociate me from dialectical-materialist psychoanalysis, just as they've usurped my orgasm theory without mentioning my name, so now the IPV is collecting its "own character analysts." I can assure you that my book was only the beginning: the real thing is still to come and cannot be mastered without me. For that, I have too much head start, namely, about ten years of extremely intensive research.

[7] Hellmuth Kaiser, author of *Effective Therapy*, published posthumously with the editorial assistance of Louis B. Fierman, M.D. See also reference to Kaiser in *Character Analysis*, pp. 315-316.

Now don't be angry about this chat, dear Lotte L. I have great confidence in you, and no "intuition" that warns me against it. I showed your letter to E. to explain the difference between true friendly criticism and the other kind. You basically understand the process and a part of my personal difficulties without taking advantage of them. But please be less trusting if you wish to avoid bitter disappointments.

Affectionately yours,

(signed) WILHELM REICH

(*Reich to Liebeck*)

January 15, 1935

Dear Lotte L.:

Ever since I decided to stick strictly to my work, I've begun to perceive the whole emptiness, waste and injustice of the entire conflict. You're right in pursuing a straight line by working through Sigmund's theory. The only constructive thing one can do today is to analyze the nature and origin of the "split" with complete intellectual honesty and independence. I've done my part—and that's the end of it. I scarcely have time to carry on this controversy. The experiments are about to begin, the character-analytic seminar is starting, and, besides, I have other things to worry about: it will be very difficult to work out, unaided, the abundance of problems presented by the clinical aspects of character analysis. Every day I run into new technical questions, which in turn give rise to new theoretical questions. I realize more and more how sinful the death-instinct theory really is. What a choking off of life itself! Meanwhile I've had my congress lecture, "Psychic Contact and Vegetative Current," typed up. You and Prag will each get a copy. Could you study it together with your colleagues and gradually start the collective work by making constructive criticism before I publish the paper? That would be a real beginning. I don't intend to publish one comprehensive paper on the problem but to work it out successively in monographs. Thus I hope to establish, in the predictable future, a detailed basis for my concept of the two kinds of work performance whose differentiation is so important.

One more thing: Nic H.[8] had the idea that we should start thinking about ways and means of protecting character-analytic technique from unwelcome distortions. What do you think? How should we go about it? I think it's important to start soon —this is bound to become a fad. We would have to establish definite training requirements. I'll never permit the work to get out of my hands: it is my strongest weapon. Please write me about this. It is also in the interest of the younger colleagues. Under no circumstances will I allow the IPV, after the way they treated me, to "practice" their own character analysis.[9]

I completely share your opinion about the "Three Contributions,"[1] with two exceptions: genitality is completely left out, and I consider his theory of the constitution to be inaccurate. By

---

[8] Nic Hoel.

[9] "Some psychoanalysts stole my principle of character-analysis without mentioning me, because to mention me as the originator of the character-analytic technique would mean to defend the orgasm theory, and to stand the blows which follow in its path. So they have thrown out the orgasm theory and are taking over a kind of ghost which does not mean yes or no, black or white, mah nor bah. You are helpless against such procedure on the part of the so-called common or little man who grabs where he can take without being punished, and pays tribute to where he is treated in an authoritative manner. Take, hit and run is their motto." Reich, from a letter to A. S. Neill, June 24, 1944.

[1] Liebeck had stated that Freud's Three Contributions to the Theory of Sex contained "just about everything that can basically be said on the subject! Everything else strikes me as mere elaboration."

the way, our circle has translated the book into Danish. I've written the preface for the translation.

I had a letter from Edith which I didn't like. I won't answer it, either. It's the old story: I "promised"—to let myself be quietly slaughtered. Just because it would have been more convenient to the Ediths and their ilk, to spare them any pangs of conscience. . . .

I would like to know who in your circle would be a serious candidate for the rigorous problems of character work and the orgasm theory.

Very cordially,
(signed) W. REICH

(Reich to F. Deutsch)[2]

Oslo, January 21, 1935

Dear Doctor:

I am extremely sorry that I did not recall the paper you sent me. But please do not forget the difficult conditions under which I have had to work in the past two years. In my paper (which is only part of a series of contributions on "personal sex-economy") I was not interested in taking a stand on the concepts of psychophysical interrelations. I would not presume to undertake such a critique. The way I see it, my only task is to develop my orgasm theory in whatever direction the facts will take it. So, for the moment, all I can do is constructive research. As for the available literature, I can only say—and this also applies to your paper—that it does not deal with the orgastic func-

[2] Felix Deutsch (1884-1964), internist, interested in psychosomatic research.

tion. Now I happen to have a "prejudice" in that the orgasm problem might hold the key to the most basic questions, provided we are sufficiently capable of mastering it. But we are still far from it. I did not even succeed in arousing any interest in it for use in clinical psychoanalysis. If I may be permitted to point out other characteristics of my work which distinguish it from other, pertinent literature, I would first of all call attention to the connection between sexuality and vegetative anxiety rooted in the orgasm function, which I stressed as early as 1926; furthermore, the conscious application of dialectical-materialist methodology to psychology and physiology. I know that the concept of psychophysical functional identity is gaining more and more ground. However, I postulate a different concept: *identity simultaneously with antithesis,* which is a problem for dialectical materialism and will have to be developed from the concrete facts. In a forthcoming paper I have carried this thought into the characterological field. You will no doubt be interested to learn that Oslo's physiological and psychological institutes have declared their readiness to help me in mastering these problems. Beginning next week, the hypothesis of the electrophysiological nature of the orgasm and of sexuality in general, developed from the clinical application of analysis and character analysis, will be tested experimentally. I think it is important not only to assert that both psychophysical parallelism and the mechanistic interaction theory are wrong while the unitary (plus antithesis) concept seems to point in the right direction: above and beyond this, we must prove experimentally what this unity *demonstrably* consists of. I believe I have been successful in respect to the detailed functions of the parasympathetic and sympathetic systems (sexuality and anxiety). But under the circumstances I do not see how today's psychoanalytic concept of anxiety is at all tenable. Perhaps I am mistaken in this respect.

I would be grateful for any criticism or suggestion; also, for a review of my work in a scientific journal. The problems on which all of us are working together will require a much greater effort and will not be solved without overcoming a great deal of confusion.

With best regards,

Yours,

(signed) WILHELM REICH

(*Reich to Liebeck*)

February 5, 1935

Dear Lotte L.:

You will be interested in my brief account that characterizes the therapeutic situation in the IPV. It is staggering, typical, almost the rule. I believe I wrote you that I took over someone who had been in analysis for three and a half years, with Kempner, Pfister and finally with Fen.[3] (for eight months), successively. This is a young, basically life-affirming girl who told me that she kept taking veronal—capriciously and out of spite—to show F. what she thought of him. F. developed tremendous anxiety, and the more he did, the more frequently she lived out her revenge in this form. Today she had her first session. I immediately noticed what three or four years ago I probably would not have seen till much later: rigid body attitude, stiff as a board, arms stretched out, hands folded, head practically nailed down. In speaking, the lips hardly moved, the voice without res-

[3] Fenichel.

onance, high-pitched, near inaudible. In previous analyses she had always insisted that she could not, and would not, speak: for three and a half years. The more she was urged to talk, the less she could do so. With F. she was silent for months, and so was he. Instead of making her aware of her body attitude, and nothing else, he asked her to change position (i.e., Ferenczi's active technique); thereupon increased defiance. The first thing I tell her is: "You're behaving as if you were facing an operation —completely stiff." Her reply: "I've never been afraid of operations; on the contrary, I've always wanted them." (Masochism!!!) I slowly begin to describe her attitude, feature by feature: mouth, voice, posture, masklike face, head virtually nailed down. After about fifteen minutes she starts speaking softly and urgently, and suddenly remembers the *anxiety* she felt as a child about operations. That she was always stretched out so expectantly; that at one time she was very angry with her mother because under some pretext she took her to a doctor without telling her the truth. It had hurt a great deal. The posture stiffened even more. I have an idea: "Corpse." I tell her that a single word seems to me to describe her attitude, but that I will not mention it because she would have to begin to feel it herself. Her reply: "Were you thinking of corpse?" Then come memories: once her hair got stuck in a crate while she was playing; she would go wild if someone suddenly grasped her from behind. The "nailed-down" head gradually acquired meaning, but I said nothing and merely continued describing her attitude. At the end of the hour she said "I don't like my back. I'm lying here as if I were glued down, as if I had no back, as if I'd been cut in two lengthwise," etc. Now what do you say to that? Not once in three years of analysis did she remember that she was afraid of surgery. Her very *attitude* communicated this. I confess

I was shaken. Three years of money, effort, life itself!!! I'm pleased, and a little proud, to have found a way. No, I would be sinning against myself if I failed to draw the therapeutic line vis-à-vis the others, cautiously, but sharply and resolutely all the same.

Which reminds me: Elsa[4] wrote me·that she cannot verbalize in her analysis. I forgot to tell you that she has characteristic mouth movements. She will not talk, or talk poorly, unless her neck cramps are made conscious to her first. Please watch this. Each silence—and this I've learned only recently—is rooted in anxiety bound up in tensions of the neck musculature. Very important for the beginning; may save months of effort if properly handled.

That's all for today!

> Affectionately,
> (signed) WILH. REICH

(*Reich to Liebeck*)

Oslo, March 11, 1935

Dear Lotte L.:

. . . .

I feel you're doing character analysis an injustice if you believe that it is merely catharsis, combined with a thorough working through, that makes it something new. The old could only be freshly re-created because I succeeded in discovering *the armor* and its structure as a fact. I've come to realize more and more that the orgasm theory not only has established a new branch of science but—above and beyond this—many old concepts have either become untenable or must undergo complete revision.

4 Elsa Lindenberg.

This could well be discussed at length and in detail. I can't deny that I sometimes feel dizzy when I gaze at the new vistas and at the uncertainties involving the mastery of the tasks ahead. A while ago it occurred to me that I might tackle the problem of the prophylaxis of neuroses in concrete practice, in a kindergarten where I would study the emotional freezing of children by direct observation and find ways of preventing it. This seems to me entirely feasible. . . .

About your last question: I, too, have at times great difficulties in the termination of treatments. I also believe that you should continue working on the development of your own self.

The equipment will arrive in a week and I hope I'll be able to demonstrate the first concrete results within a few months. . . .

(signed) REICH

(*Reich to Liebeck*)

March 30, 1935

Dear Lotte L.:

This is my first chance to answer your letter in greater detail. Your letters are a great pleasure. You and Schjelderup are the first analysts—may I say, character analysts—whose results show the true nature of character-analytic work. What you described in your cases has long been familiar to me, although up to now I haven't been able to master all of it theoretically: the shattering insight into the previous wasteland of living and just existing; the tremendous fear of happiness; the reactivation of the deepest—I would say, almost biological—reactions such as bursting; the timidity in coming to grips with reality in a healthy way, etc.

From the terminal stages of clinical cases I first came to understand the world's fear of the orgasm theory and, even more, its lack of understanding, which reflects a repression of its better judgment. Life doesn't become any easier when one begins to feel things might be different. . . .

I would appreciate it if you would elaborate your criticism of Freud in detail. The other day, after a long interval, I was scanning the "Three Contributions," and I was amazed by some of the passages, especially on genitality. I've done myself a grave injustice by working for so many years under the impression that my theory of genitality was rooted in Freud. This was merely due to my father fixation. Some day I hope to make a clean break.

Gerö was here and caused a lot of trouble. So long as he knew he was structurally unsuited for holding a concept and fighting for it, all was well. But then he began to have illusions. He broke some rules of conventional politeness toward me—clearly the result of a bad conscience—and his lecture to the group was poorly received.

Yesterday Fenichel presented his "criticism" of my technique and everybody was against him, including most of his own analysands (Nic, Raknes). Did you know he's leaving Oslo? Things have been hard for him lately because the superiority of character analysis had become obvious to all. He's going to Prague. Unfortunately, he believes that this will solve his problems. The whole Norwegian group has sided with me, except for one who doesn't know what it is all about, and two who're honestly trying but are structurally incapable. Since the last discussion I haven't been to the Association, but all of them are attending my lectures and my character seminar (where Mote, by the way, acquitted himself brilliantly).

Now about the equipment: I have to start very slowly and work my way into the electrophysiological technique. It will be very hard but looks most promising. The apparatus is among the most modern there is. It may soon be necessary to have a professionally trained assistant come from Germany because the local physiologist merely wants to "help," but that's not enough. The first experiments (recording of potentials at erogenous zones) will start soon. Further experimentation, however, will have to develop from whatever course the work takes. Please try to find an unemployed electrophysiologist who is fully acquainted with the oscillograph and knows about the physiology of the skin and the vegetative nervous system.

. . . .

Keep well. Cordially,

(signed) REICH

(Reich to Freud)

May 20, 1935
Dr. Wilhelm Reich
Oslo/Norway
Drammensveien 110 h

Prof. Dr. Sigm. Freud
Vienna IX .
Berggasse 19

My dear Professor:
I am enclosing a pamphlet containing my lecture at the XIIth Psychoanalytic Congress, in expanded form. I was able to give this lecture only as a guest of the IPV.

Several years ago, when I reported on the role of the orgastic function in the psychic economy, you told me that either I had regressed to the pre-analytic level with its denial of pregenitality or, if this was not the case, that I would some day have to carry the heavy burden of psychoanalysis alone. I do not know if you remember this. I was extremely impressed with your comment. Since the first part of your observation does not apply, the second has all the better anticipated a glimpse of the future.

I would appreciate it if you would convince yourself, by reading my pamphlet, that I have sincerely tried not to turn the grave injustice I suffered into grounds for a personal and irrational reaction. I hope that, at least in this respect, I have succeeded.

I also believe that in this paper I was more successful than before in explaining the clinical reasons that compelled me to clarify the contradictions which today dominate the doctrine of psychoanalysis. Furthermore, I feel that I was able to find a constructive formulation for the common roots as well as for the theoretical differences inherent in this contradiction.

With best wishes,

Very respectfully yours,
(signed) WILHELM REICH

(Reich to English)

O. Spurgeon English*
255 So. 17th Street
Philadelphia, Pa.

Oslo, August 14, 1937

Dear Dr. English:

. . . .

That American psychoanalysts do not understand the essence of character analysis does not surprise me. Character analysis is not supposed to be a continuance of Freud's technique but originated from the criticism of the interpretational technique while consistently developing the resistance analysis. Please do not regard Dr. Rado and Dr. Horney as being in the least representative of the character-analytic trend. I am enclosing a prospectus of articles which you may order from the publisher direct.

The biological department of our institute is constantly growing. The forthcoming issue of our Journal, which is now available, will tell you about the direction this work is taking.

I would greatly appreciate it if you could let me have the names and professions as well as the addresses of young colleagues who are interested in the continued development of character analysis.

If you should come to Europe next year, I hope you will stop off at Oslo.

I would be pleased to hear from you again.

With kindest regards,

Yours,

(signed) REICH

* American psychiatrist who studied with Reich in Europe.

Oslo, November 24, 1937

Dr. O. S. English
255 So. 17th Street
Philadelphia

Dear Dr. English:

I acknowledge with thanks your letter of October 29th together with your check for . . .

I would be pleased if you could send me a copy of your recent book for review in our Journal.

Now I have the following request: Several psychiatrists here are currently attacking psychoanalysis in general, and my development of character analysis in particular. Next week there will be a big conference of the psychiatric association where our people—the sex-economic therapists together with the psychoanalysts—will oppose these attacks. Basically, this struggle also involves recognition by organized medicine [of our work] and training. Our friends will argue that both structural psychology of the neuroses and sexual theory are being taught in many psychiatric institutions the world over—for example, in your own—but that certain psychiatric groups are still rejecting these new insights, sometimes with hostility, just as it happened twenty or thirty years ago. Now it would greatly assist our friends if you wrote up a factual letter that you, being the head of a psychiatric clinic and professor of psychiatry, have first-hand knowledge of the technique of character analysis, if only at its incipient stage, and that you are teaching analytic structural psychology to your students. I do not know if your position over there permits you to make this gesture. Please write me frankly about it. Such a letter would have to be here by Christmas.

Here is an example of the tactics employed by some psychiatrists. In his attack on me, Professor Ragnar Vogt thinks he can draw on the anthropologist Bronislaw Malinowski for support. Now we can prove conclusively that Malinowski approves both my ethnological interpretations of his book [*Rest of sentence missing Ed.*]. Furthermore, he himself has disputed the biological roots of the child-parent conflict, and has interpreted it sociologically. I do not know if you are fully familiar with this struggle in the Psychoanalytic Association, and outside of it, in 1926. If not, you might be interested in reading the back issues of "Imago" for 1926-27 on Malinowski's views—of course, only if you consider such orientation necessary and feel that the avenues of approach you studied with me in Vienna and Berlin are insufficiently enlightening.

I would very much appreciate your writing me more often and in greater detail about your differences of opinion with other analysts. You know my own stand, as well as the difficulties of defending the scientific, sexual-theoretical basis of analytic psychologists against the theorists of the death instinct and those scholars who reject the scientific premise.

With kindest regards,

Yours,

(signed) REICH

(Statement by Malinowski) *
The London School of Economics and Political Science
(University of London)
Houghton Street,
Aldwych,
London, W .C. 2.

DEPARTMENT OF ANTHROPOLOGY

12th March, 1938

To those whom it may concern:

I have known Dr. Wilhelm Reich for five years, during which period I have read his works and also on many occasions had the opportunity of conversation and discussion with him, in London and Oslo. Both through his published work and in the personal contacts he has impressed me as an original and sound thinker, a genuine personality, and a man of open character and courageous views. I regard his sociological work a distinct and valuable contribution to Science. It would, in my opinion, be the greatest loss if Dr. Reich were in any way prevented from enjoying the fullest facilities for the working out of his ideas and scientific discoveries.

I should like to add that my testimonial may have some additional strength, coming as it does from one who does not share Dr. Reich's advanced views nor yet his sympathies with Marxian philosophy—I like to describe myself as an old-fashioned, almost conservative liberal.

B . MALINOWSKI
Professor of Anthropology in the
University of London, Member of the
Royal Academy of Holland (Amsterdam)

* All of Malinowski's letters were written in English.

(Reich to Malinowski)

Oslo, April 29, 1938

Dear Bronislaw:

Many thanks for your letter of April 25th, which gave us all great pleasure. In the past two weeks we've had a very hard time. A couple of sex know-it-alls attacked my paper on "The Bions," without knowledge of the subject matter and in an absolutely disgraceful manner. This caused a storm in the press, pro and con. As a result, I've leaped ahead by at least ten years. Now the question of sex-economy along with the bions is hitting the world press. I didn't ask for this, but now that it has happened it's a good thing.

I'm not an incorrigible optimist, but thanks to my work I have deeply experienced not only man's satanic impulses but also the human side of him. So if Hitler plucks the strings of the subhuman theme, why shouldn't we concentrate on his human core which we know exists all along but has merely been buried?

. . . We think of you often and fondly. Please write as often as you can.

With affectionate regards,

yours,

(signed) WILHELM REICH

(*Malinowski to Reich*)

Ellen Emerson House
Smith College
Northampton, Mass.
July 21, 1939

My dear Willy:

Many thanks for your letter of July 10. As you can see, I am still in America, and I shall be only too happy to do all I can to help you.

Unfortunately it is by no means easy to manipulate matters now, owing to the enormous pressure on the universities and teaching institutions here. The other unfortunate point in your case is the fact that many psychoanalysts will have nothing to do with you. You know where my sympathies are, so I need not tell you how indignant I feel when this attitude is revealed. This would not be so bad if American psychoanalysts were not so much dominated by people from Vienna or Berlin. But wherever can there be a psychoanalytical society with Rank or H. Sachs or Alexander in the key position.

I shall see, however, whether I shall not be able to do something. Since Dr. Wolfe has not gotten in touch with me, I am writing him a line. If I can do anything I shall write you.

Yours always,

(signed) B. MALINOWSKI

I am also writing to my friend Alvin Johnson of the New School of Social Research and to one or two influential friends at Johns Hopkins.

B.M.

Oslo, 1939

Dr. Scharfenberg
Chief Resident Physician
Oslo

Before moving to New York, I am taking the liberty to express my heartfelt thanks for the service you have rendered my scientific work. I would beg you to restrain your amazement over this somewhat unusual gesture. I am very much in earnest, for I have learned to appreciate the enormously important role of antagonists. The antagonist himself is usually unaware of this aspect of his achievement. You have *advanced* my extremely difficult scientific work by at least a decade. A British scholar recently remarked that "the whole scientific world was now talking about the bions." He added that I was crazy, but nevertheless the world *must talk* about them and can no longer silence them to death.

I found it intellectually gratifying to discover that so-called convictions are a dime a dozen but that real actions are dangerous. You pretend to fight alcoholism and, if I remember rightly, you belong to several temperance societies. Now it may have escaped your notice that the case history you referred to with such abusive vehemence describes *the cure of an alcoholic* by means of the recently developed vegetotherapy. The damming up of sexual energy and the resultant vegetative anxiety are very likely the most important underlying causes of alcoholism. It is known that alcohol has a vagotonic effect on sympatheticotonic anxiety, i.e., it resolves anxiety and depression. The effect of alcohol can be permanently canceled out through natural orgastic

[5] This letter was not sent. It carries the following notation in Reich's hand: "Leave the idiot be. *But*, the idiots govern the world!"

gratification. But to you, the enemy of alcohol, "morality" was more important than a new scientific explanation of alcoholism. The enormity of such an insight can only be appreciated if we consider that medicine's fight against nationwide epidemics must face not only disease itself but also the impact of such authoritarian influences.

Furthermore, it became clear as never before that the exponents of the obsolete school of psychiatry are determined to collaborate with the *police*, while modern psychiatry works with the *patient*. You reacted to the modern treatment of the difficult problem of infantile onanism with police denunciations, while we work with kindergarten and teaching staffs in order to remove for all time a medieval inquisition that has eroded the vital energies of small children. Since you and your school of thought—if such it can be called—are *silent* on practical suggestions, and since we regard the police approach to sexual misery as a corroding endemic disease, the advantages are unquestionably on our side. We enjoy the affirmative support of the people's innate vitality. Over the long haul, practitioners who threaten with deportation proceedings are fighting a losing battle. You know that it was psychiatrists of your own persuasion who conspired to make my residence in Denmark and Sweden impossible, and that local and foreign fascists openly cheered your opinions about me. That this scandalizing exposure could happen to a member of a workers' party calling itself socialist, to a registered member of the Friends of the Right of Asylum, to an "anti-fascist," etc., was worth witnessing, in spite of embarrassing inconveniences. It proves the close ties between fascist ideology and the false premises inherent in genetic-oriented psychiatry. Even Freud battled against the all-too-easy trend to "explain away" the sexual troubles of youth and the nightmares of frustrated women by unexplored genes. From the "theory of degenerative genetic substances" to Hitler's "racial theory," it is only one step. True science will stop the influence of such atrophied thinking. In the history of science your name will go down on the *minus* side. And yet, you might be grateful to me in turn: thanks to your active opposition to me, you have gained the honor that sometime in the future you will at least be mentioned negatively in the history of science.

(signed) WILHELM REICH, M.D.

(*Malinowski to Reich*)

January 31, 1942

128 H.G.S.

Yale University

Department of Anthropology

New Haven, Connecticut

Dr. Wilhelm Reich

99-06 69th Avenue

Forest Hills, New York

My dear Willi:

I am delighted to hear that your difficulties with the immigration people have been resolved completely and favorably. The whole matter, of course, was ridiculous since no one in his senses can suspect you of pro-Nazi sympathies or leanings. Nevertheless, such things are most disturbing.[6]

[6] On December 12, 1941, at two o'clock in the morning, Reich "was routed from bed by agents of the FBI (Federal Bureau of Investigation) and taken to Ellis Island. It was perfectly clear, from Reich's record as well as from investigations carried on both prior to the arrest and afterwards, that there

I am writing these few lines to let you know at once how delighted I am that this unnecessary disturbance is over. I hope also to see you quite soon and shall make a special point of getting in touch with you.

Yours always,

(signed) B. MALINOWSKI

(*Reich to Malinowski*)[7]

(n.d.)

My dear Bronislaw,

I was able to answer letters and such things first today, more than three weeks after my release from Ellis Island. They had investigated my "case" for more than a year, found nothing, had no complaints, and yet I was behind bars for three and a half weeks. The whole thing was completely irrational, due to some denunciation by some coward who dares not oppose me in the open field of free discussion. My first wife has something to do with it. My daughter Lore told me several months ago that I had better watch out because her mother had, together with Dr. Kubie from the Psa. Society, prepared something against me in case that I don't behave well. Here you are! Do you remember my troubles in Denmark and Sweden back in 1934 when psychiatrists had run to the police? Well, here's the same story. The odds confronting our work are tremendous, but so are also the achievements. A book of mine, "The Discovery of the Orgone,"

---

was nothing whatsoever to incriminate Reich under the Enemy Alien Act. It took until January 5, 1942, to effect his unconditional release. Though denunciations with the police as a weapon against Reich's work had happened before in Europe, it had never come to an arrest." T. P. Wolfe, in a note to the Translator's Preface of *The Function of the Orgasm*, p. xix.

[7] Minor grammatical corrections have been made in this letter. Reich, at this time, was just beginning to write in English.

summarizing the past twenty years of biophysical and character-analytic research is coming soon in English, and so does a Journal issued by our Institut and the American branch.

I wish to thank you for your affidavit which you sent on the occasion of my arrest. I really look forward to seeing you sometime soon. I hope you are well and not too much distressed about the international disaster. I think the psychiatrists who understand distorted biological functioning in the human beings will have to accomplish hard tasks once this is over.

Always yours,
(signed) REICH

(Hitschmann to Reich)

June 18, 1942
57 Brattle Street
Cambridge, Mass.

Dear Dr. Reich:

It was only today, forwarded from London, that I received the first issue of your new periodical,[8] which I will read immediately and thoroughly, together with the English version of *The Function of the Orgasm.*

Just recently I was able to cure a young woman with severe anxiety and strong depersonalization symptoms by restoring her orgastic potency. For the first time I heard her talk of her frequent night orgasms and her dreams about the sex act with her husband.

For twelve years I've now lived here with my capable wife—

---

[8] *International Journal for Sex-Economy and Orgone-Research.*

my daughter is married and in New York—right in the sticks, that's how little psychoanalytic knowledge and achievement you find around here.

Freud's works untranslated; Fenichel's out of print; no analysis in the hospitals, which have to be content with "guessing at psychodynamics."

Life and work and more knowledge than others are my daily source of pleasure.

With best regards,

Yours,

(signed) H I T S C H M A N N

(*Reich to Hitschmann*)

June 20, 1942

ORGONE AND CANCER RESEARCH LABORATORY

Forest Hills, New York

Dear Dr. Hitschmann:

I was very pleased with your letter, for I often think of the important and stimulating years, back in the twenties, when we battled for the Vienna Psychiatric Clinic. Since then so many difficult and tragic things have happened, to society, to my work and to my person. You happen to be one of the very few psychoanalysts who do not recoil from the fact that the libido discovered by our teacher Freud is now both tangible and measurable as biologically efficacious orgone energy. It never fails to amaze me how little the true scientific principle of emotional energy has been grasped and applied.

The journal and the book will show you that we have not only remained loyal to Freud's good old doctrines but have also supplied "*depth* psychology" with the necessary *depth*. Your critique of the over-all situation is quite correct. Maybe this will change some day, thanks to the young science of biophysics which grew out of analytic thinking. It will be a long and hard struggle; people are after all terrified of Nature.

I am glad you managed to escape from hell. My own life is still difficult, full of hostile attacks and dangerous incidents, but I may say that I am fully compensated by the fruits of my scientific research. With best regards, and please remember me to your wife.

Yours,

(signed) REICH

(*Reich to A. S. Neill*)[9]

December 9, 1948

My dear Neill:

We just received your letter. Yes, my work has burst open everywhere and it is now rather much to handle, since I feel quite like in a desert with no real, active, eager, fighting helpers around. There is some basic hesitancy or reluctance to stand up clearly and faithfully for our work and to defend it in public just as eagerly as the enemies of this work are attacking it by defamation. The latest news is that some psychoanalysts apparently ran to the District Attorney to stop my work. They pulled out some law from the books which said that whoever directs mental-hygiene work must be licensed to do so, or something similar. This is, of course, nonsense, since I am the one who licenses

[9] A. S. Neill, educator, headmaster of Summerhill, Leiston, England. This is an excerpt of a letter written in English.

doctors and educators to practice what I found and teach. I would appreciate it highly if you would make it widely known that the psychoanalysts and some psychiatrists who have no answer to my work are cowardly enough to use defamation, distortion and denunciation.

There is no doubt about it, as we have found out lately, through many witnesses who have sworn to their written statements, that there is a concerted effort on the part of the New York Psychoanaly. Association to smash my work by denunciation. For instance, the rumor was circulated about two weeks ago in many places that a woman patient had been masturbated at the Orgone Institute and thereupon had a breakdown. The woman whose name was mentioned in this connection had never been here. We went after this story immediately with the help of our lawyer,[1] and the man who spread the rumor, a Dr. Miller, took it back immediately. Well, this is what I call plague.

. . . .

All my best to all of you,
(signed) REICH

[1] See Memorandum, p.

2) EMOTIONAL PLAGUE:

The psychoanalysts

Regarding Fenichel and the schizophrenia rumor [1]

"I shall cite another example, one in which the projection mechanism of the emotional plague, in the form of defamation, is even more clearly evident. Back in Norway, I heard that a rumor was going around to the effect that I had developed schizophrenia and had spent some time in a mental institution. When I came to the United States in 1939, I found that this rumor had become widespread in this country, even more so than in Europe, where my work was better known. It soon became evident that the rumor emanated from the same European source, a person who had since moved to America.

The situation did not lack a certain irony: This person, shortly after my break with the Psychoanalytic Association, had suffered a nervous breakdown and had to spend some weeks in a mental institution. The accident of the nervous breakdown ap-

[1] *Character Analysis*, pp. 269–271.

parently gave the later rumor-monger quite a shock. At that time, he found himself in a difficult conflict: On the one hand, he realized the correctness of my scientific development; on the other hand, he was incapable of breaking with his organization which had come into sharp conflict with my development. As is apt to happen in such cases, he grasped the opportunity of diverting attention from himself to me, who at that time was in the center of dangerous and widespread polemics. He was convinced that I was hopelessly lost, and the temptation to give me an additional push was too great. His reaction was a projection according to the specific pattern of the emotional plague. *I had never been psychotic or in a mental institution.* Rather, I have carried the heaviest burden to this day without disturbances of my capacity for work and for love.

After all, a mental disease is not in itself a disgrace. Like any decent psychiatrist, I have deep sympathy for mental patients and often even admiration for their conflicts. A mental patient is much more serious, much closer to living functioning, than a Babbitt or a socially dangerous plague-ridden individual. This defamation was intended to ruin me and my work. It led to some dangerous and difficult situations. For example, in many students I had at that time the additional task of convincing them that I was *not* psychotic. In certain phases of orgone therapy, a specific mechanism of the emotional plague makes its appearance in a typical manner: As soon as the patient or student comes in contact with his plasmatic currents, he develops severe orgasm anxiety. In this phase, the orgone therapist is considered a 'dirty, sexual swine' or as 'crazy.' I emphasize the fact that this reaction occurs in *all* cases. Now, most of the students had heard of the rumor in question. The theory of sex-economy is in many ways so revolutionary that it is very easy to call it 'crazy.' It must be said that, as a result of this rumor, complicated situations became such as to be a danger to life. Such consequences of a plague reaction should be made impossible by all available legal means. I owe it only to my clinical experience that I was able to master the dangers resulting from this rumor."

Excerpt from a letter by Harry Obeymeyer to Theodore P. Wolfe, M.D.

Tel Aviv, Israel
Oct. 16, 1943

For the last 2 or 3 yrs Dr. Reich has been talked about in this country as having been in a mental asylum. I never bothered about this nonsense as the irrational make-up of this sort of slandering was too obvious. Whenever someone came out with this item of news I simply showed him a letter I had from Dr. Reich. But not until recently did I succeed in tracing the "news" to its sources. The chief propagandist was the late Dr. Eitingon, a sworn enemy of Dr. Reich. Dr. E. claimed to have been informed by Mrs. Anni Reich.

This behavior on the part of psychiatrists is, to put it mildly, obnoxious. Can one do anything about it?

December 26, 1945

Dr. Richard H. Hutchings, Editor
The Psychiatric Quarterly
Utica State Hospital
Utica, N.Y.

Dear Dr. Hutchings:

In a review of Wilhelm Reich's THE SEXUAL REVOLUTION, *The Psychiatric Quarterly* 19, 1945, 717ff., I find the following statement, referring to Wilhelm Reich:

"*When he arrived at New York as a refugee, his admission to this country was long delayed while the government investigated charges against him of immorality.*"

This statement is pure fabrication. I was present at the dock when Wilhelm Reich arrived in this country. There was no delay, charge or government investigation of any kind whatsoever. A statement like the above is irresponsible and libelous.

I fully understand that you, as the Editor, cannot be expected to check up on the accuracy of statements made by your reviewers. On the other hand, if you allow reviews to be published anonymously (a policy which I cannot understand either as an editor or as a reviewer), who, then, takes the responsibility for such statements? This statement is an example of irresponsible rumor-mongering and certainly has no place in a scientific journal. I trust that you will set your readers straight in this matter.

Very sincerely yours,

(signed) THEODORE P. WOLFE, M.D.

Oslo, Sept. 29, 1948

Gabriel Langfeldt, M.D.
Psychiatric Clinic
Vinderen, Norway

I have been told by different, completely trustworthy persons that in a meeting at the Psychiatric Clinic on, I believe, the thirteenth of this month, you said that in America now it is the general opinion that Dr. Wilhelm Reich is completely insane. None of the individuals who reported this to me had written down your statements verbatim, so I cannot give you your exact words. But according to these persons this was the content of what you said.

I assume that the reports are true and I would like to ask you on what basis you make statements like these. I intend to report this to Dr. Reich so that he can take the necessary steps to protect himself against attacks of this kind.

The following is somewhat off-the-subject, but I would like to inform you that during the latter part of August and the first part of Sept. this year, I attended a conference of Reich's students and co-workers, among them seventeen doctors, most of whom were psychiatrists with long experience and some with previous and present university teaching positions. I talked very thoroughly with most of them and none of them seemed to have detected Reich's insanity.

In case you wish to add or correct any of your above-mentioned statement about Dr. Reich, I will wait till the seventh of October before I inform Reich about them.

Sincerely,

(signed) OLA RAKNES

[Dr. Langfeldt has refused permission to print his reply to Dr. Raknes, together with other correspondence on the subject with Dr. A. Allan Cott (who has also refused permission to have his letter printed). In his reply, Dr. Langfeldt gave as the source for his statement an article by Mildred Edie Brady, a free-lance writer (not a psychiatrist as he had assumed) which was published in *Harper's* in April 1947. Entitled "The Strange Case of Wilhelm Reich," it created the impression that Reich was insane. Prompted by her complaint that "the medical profession had not themselves made sufficient effort to warn the public of their non-approval of Mr. [sic] Reich," the Menninger Clinic reprinted the article in their bulletin. According to Dr. Langfeldt, those psychiatrists with whom he had discussed the article subscribed to this viewpoint. Editors.]

TO WHOM IT MAY CONCERN

I, Nic Waal, M.D., hereby report the following facts: Mitja Fabian, M.D., Psychoanalyst at the Menninger Clinic, Topeka, Kansas, said in my presence and that of Dr. Bergman, that it is long recognized that Wilhelm Reich is crazy. She was also very disturbed about the fact that Dr. Meyer Silvert intended to study with Wilhelm Reich and told Mrs. Ruth Cohen that something should be done to prevent Silvert from going to Reich, because Reich is crazy.

Dr. Karl Menninger, in a discussion with me, warned me against connecting my work with Reich's name and asked me whether the orgone business of Reich wasn't crazy. I believe

that the rumors were originated years ago by the late Dr. Otto
Fenichel.

November 9th, 1948

(signed) ————————

Nic Waal, M.D.

Dated this 9th day of November 1948
Anne Silverzweig
Notary Public, State of New York

*Memorandum given by Reich's lawyer, Arthur Garfield Hays, to
Dr. Miller's lawyer, Abraham Harris, at the conclusion of a conference with him*

December 22, 1948

RE: ORGONE INSTITUTE

Dr. Joseph S. A. Miller has made the following statement:

That Dr. Oberndorf had phoned him and had given him the
following information: That a Mrs. ———— ———— had gone to the
Orgone Institute on the recommendation of Dr. Singer, and
there had been undressed, manipulated and finally masturbated;
that she was assured that this would help her and later treatments would go even deeper.

Dr. Miller further stated that at Dr. Oberndorf's call he had
added that the patient had gone into an extreme panic for several days as a result of this examination, and that they had put
her in a box not unlike a steam box.

This story is made up out of whole cloth, is wholly untrue,
and is extremely damaging to the Orgone Institute. The same
statement had been made by Dr. Annie Rubenstein and I believe by Dr. Nunberg. My own view is that the way to clear this

thing up is for the doctors themselves to investigate the sources of this rumor. It is quite possible that Dr. Oberndorf got the story from someone else. I should expect Dr. Miller, or you his attorney, to investigate all the facts. We can prove to you that the above story is wholly untrue, and we ask you to start your investigation on that assumption. I should then expect, after running this thing down, for the doctors themselves to clear it all up, have all those involved state where they heard this story, and for the people from whom it originally emanated to state the source of their information. I should then expect an expression of regret and apology from all doctors who had anything to do with this, and assurances that they would avoid in the future spreading any rumors of fact unless they had evidence or proof of such facts. I would further suggest that the doctors state that if any such rumors come to them they make inquiries at the Orgone Institute to find out if the facts are correct before they repeat such facts.

ARTHUR GARFIELD HAYS

[In a letter dated September 17, 1950, Dr. A. Allen Cott drew Reich's attention to a book by Hervey Cleckley, M.D., entitled *The Mask of Sanity*, in which Reich was presented as a psychopathic personality. Again, the material for this conclusion was drawn from the Brady article and its endorsement by the Menninger Clinic. Also, using the *Journal* of the A.M.A. as his authority, Cleckey referred to the orgone energy accumulator as a fraudulent device and repeated the completely unfounded statement that it was intended as a means of *curing* cancer. Eds.]

In a statement in the APA[2] Newsletter of April 15, 1954, under the title "Orgone Energy Devices Barred from Interstate Commerce," appeared the following:

"The acting Medical Director of the Federal Food and Drug Administration has expressed his Agency's appreciation for APA's help in the successful development of its case."

[2] American Psychiatric Association.

3) MISCELLANEOUS

The significance of style
in psychoanalytic writing

INTRODUCTION TO "IBSEN'S PEER GYNT,
LIBIDOKONFLIKTE UND WAHNGEBILDE"
— October, 1952.

This manuscript, written by hand by Wilhelm Reich in 1919–
1920, is being deposited with the Sigmund Freud Archives not
only because it had some interest for the psychoanalytic historian. It is being deposited mainly to give an impression of the
academic atmosphere in which the early psychoanalytic movement was submerged at that time. Psychoanalysis, which dealt
with human dirt of the worst kind, and at the same time had to
survive the onslaught of the maligning, gossiping, slandering
academic world of established "sex-free" psychiatry, was forced
to compensate for the dirt it handled by a highly academic, "pu-
rified" style. It was, for example, a habit with early psychoanalytic lectures to introduce their lectures with an excuse as to
their right to deal with the subject, or as to the subject itself.

Also, the psychoanalyst sat behind the patient and the patient's eyes were covered with a piece of cloth in many cases.

This is not to depreciate early psychoanalytic procedures. It is to tell the world what pioneering effort encounters.

It is noteworthy that Freud's simple style in his first papers of the 1890's became more and more involved, academic, and "Goethean" as the decades passed by. Reich, who met psychoanalysis in 1919 and had grown up in the spirit and language of German, academic, natural science and philosophy, discloses a shrouded, academic style in this manuscript, which deals little with sex directly. Ten years later, he was engrossed in the rude, crude ways of people's sex behavior and sex lives. The academic style which he had employed in the early 1920's fell asunder. Still, it was noticeable in the first German edition of his *Mass Psychology of Fascism* (1932). But as the years passed by, and as the emotional plague increased its efforts to kill Reich's fight for the love life of infants and adolescents, in the 1930's, the style became more congruous with the contents: simple, straight, brief-sentenced, hard-hitting, direct, avoiding circumlocution, evasion, and academicism. Thus, the development of style in Reich's writing demonstrates the way whch led him, around 1930, back to where Sigmund Freud had tended in his development around 1900: *The sexual stasis neuroses in the masses of the population.* From here, also, the conflict between Sigmund Freud and Wilhelm Reich is emerging in a clearly understandable manner. The social consequences which Reich drew from the existence of sexual mass neuroses in the beginning of the twentieth century, consequences which were so severely refuted by the world at large and by the psychoanalysts in particular, did not begin to emerge widely visible on the social scene before the late 1940's when sexuality of children and genitality were openly discussed and presented in textbooks as well as in novels in the American literature. The triumph of the sex-economic development away from psychoanalysis began to be obvious.

Supplementation of Freud's theory of the anxiety neurosis[1]

As mentioned before, I came to Freud through the field of sexology. It is thus not surprising that his theory of the *actual neuroses* (*Aktualneurosen*) which I later termed *stasis neuroses* (*Stauungsneurosen*) struck me as much more in keeping with natural science than the "interpretation" of the "meaning" of symptoms in the "psychoneuroses." Freud applied the name of actual neuroses to neuroses which resulted from present-day (*aktuelle*) disturbances of sex life. According to this concept, anxiety neurosis and neurasthenia were disturbances which lacked a "psychic etiology." Instead, they were the *immediate* result of dammed-up sexuality. They were like toxic disturbances. Freud assumed the existence of *"chemical sexual substances"* which, if not correctly "metabolized," caused such symptoms as palpitation, cardiac irregularity, acute anxiety attacks, sweating and other vegetative symptoms. He did not establish a connection between anxiety neurosis and the vegetative system. Anxiety neurosis, so his clinical experience showed, was caused by sexual abstinence or coitus interruptus. It had to be distinguished from neurasthenia, which, in contradistinction, was caused by "sexual abuse," such as excessive masturbation, and which was characterized by pain in the back, headaches, general irritability, disturbances of memory and concentration,

[1] *The Function of the Orgasm*, pp. 66-72.

etc. That is, Freud classified *according to their etiology* syndromes which official neurology and psychiatry did not understand. For this, he was attacked by the psychiatrist Lowenfeld, who, like hundreds of other psychiatrists, denied completely the sexual etiology of the neuroses. Freud was trying to adapt his concepts to clinical terminology. As he put it, the symptoms of the actual neuroses, in contrast to those of the *psychoneuroses,* especially hysteria and compulsion neurosis, betrayed no psychic content whatsoever. The symptoms of the latter always had a tangible content, *also always of a sexual nature.* Only, the concept of sexuality had to be taken in a broad sense. At the bottom of every psychoneurosis was the incest phantasy and the fear of injury to the genital. They were, indeed, *infantile* and *unconscious* sexual ideas which expressed themselves in the psychoneurotic symptom. Freud made a very sharp distinction between actual neuroses and psychoneuroses. The psychoneuroses, understandably, occupied the center of the clinical interest of the psychoanalyst. According to Freud, the treatment of the actual neuroses consisted in the elimination of the harmful sexual practices, such as sexual abstinence or coitus interruptus in anxiety neurosis, excessive masturbation in neurasthenia. The psychoneuroses, on the other hand, called for psychoanalytic treatment. In spite of this sharp distinction, Freud admitted a connection between the two. He thought it likely that every psychoneurosis centered around an "actual-neurotic core." This illuminating statement, which Freud never followed up, was the starting point of my own investigations of stasis anxiety.

In the actual neurosis in Freud's sense, biological energy is misdirected; it is blocked from access to consciousness and motility. The anxiety (*Aktualangst*) and the immediate vegetative symptoms are, as it were, malignant growths which are nourished by the undischarged sexual energy. But, on the other hand, the peculiar psychic manifestations of hysterias and compulsion neuroses also looked like biologically meaningless malignant growths. Where did *they* derive their energy from? Undoubtedly from the "actual-neurotic core" of the dammed-up sexual energy. This, and nothing else, could be the *source of energy* in the psychoneurosis. No other interpretation would fit Freud's suggestion. However, the majority of psychoanalysts opposed Freud's theory of the actual neuroses. They contended *that actual neuroses did not exist at all;* that these disturbances, also, were "psychically determined"; that even in the so-called "free-floating anxiety" unconscious psychic contents could be demonstrated. The chief exponent of this view was Stekel. He, like others, failed to see the fundamental difference between psychosomatic affect and psychic content of a symptom. In other words, it was quite generally contended that every kind of anxiety and nervous disturbance was of *psychic* origin, and *not of somatic* origin, as Freud had assumed for the actual neuroses. Freud never resolved this contradiction, but he continued to adhere to his distinction between the two groups of neuroses. Notwithstanding the general assertions as to the non-existence of anxiety neurosis, I saw such cases in great numbers in the psychoanalytic clinic. However, the symptoms of the actual neuroses had undeniably a psychic *superstructure. Pure* actual neuroses are rare. The distinction was not as sharp as Freud had assumed. Such specialized questions may seem unimportant to the layman. But it will be shown that they contained decisive problems of human health.

There could be no doubt: *The psychoneuroses had an actual-*

neurotic core and the actual neuroses had a psychoneurotic su-perstructure. Was there any sense in making the distinction? Was it not just a matter of a quantitative difference?

While most analysts ascribed everything to the psychic content of the neurotic symptoms, leading psychopathologists, like Jaspers, contended that psychological interpretation of meaning, and thus, psychoanalysis, were not within the realm of natural science at all. The "meaning" of a psychic attitude or action, they said, could be comprehended only in terms of philosophy, and not of natural science. Natural science dealt only with *quantities* and energies, philosophy with psychic *qualities*; and there was no bridge between the quantitative and the qualitative. It was plainly a matter of the question whether or not psychoanalysis and its method belonged to natural science. In other words: *Is a scientific psychology in the strict sense of the word at all possible?* Can psychoanalysis claim to be such a psychology? Or is it only one of the many philosophical schools? Freud himself paid no attention to these methodological questions and quietly continued to publish his clinical observations; he disliked philosophical discussions. But I had to fight such arguments on the part of un-understanding antagonists. They tried to classify us as mystics and thus to settle the question. But we knew that—for the first time in the history of psychology—we were engaging in *natural science.* We wanted to be taken seriously. It was only in the hard-fought controversies over these questions that the sharp weapons were forged with which I later was able to defend Freud's cause. If it were true that only experimental psychology in the sense of Wundt was "natural science," because it measured human reactions quantitatively, then, I thought, something was wrong with natural science. For Wundt and his pupils knew nothing of the human in his living reality. They evaluated him according to the number of seconds he needed to react to the word "dog." They still do. We, on the other hand, evaluated a person according to the manner in which he handled his conflicts in life, and the motives which activated him. To me, there loomed behind this argument the more important question as to whether it might be possible to arrive at a concrete formulation of Freud's concept of *"psychic energy,"* or whether it might be possible even to subsume it under the general concept of energy.

Philosophical arguments cannot be countered with facts. The Viennese philosopher and physiologist Allers refused to enter upon the question of the existence of an unconscious psychic life, on the grounds that the assumption of an "unconscious" was *"a priori* erroneous from a philosophical point of view." I hear similar objections today. When I assert that highly sterilized substances produce life, it is argued that the slide was dirty, or that, if there seems to be life, it is "only a matter of Brownian movement." The fact that it is very easy to distinguish dirt on the slide from the bions, and equally easy to distinguish Brownian movement from vegetative movement, is not taken into consideration. In brief, "objective science" is a problem in itself.

In this confusion, I was unexpectedly aided by such everyday clinical observations as the ones provided by the two patients mentioned above. Gradually it became clear that *the intensity of an idea depends upon the somatic excitation* with which it is connected. Emotions originate from the instincts, consequently from the *somatic* sphere. Ideas, on the other hand, certainly are a definitely "psychic," "non-somatic" thing. *What, then, is the connection between the "non-somatic" idea and the "somatic" excitation?* For example, the idea of sexual intercourse is vivid and forceful if one is in a state of full sexual excitation. For some time after sexual gratification, however, it cannot be vividly reproduced; it is dim, colorless, and vague. Just here must the secret of the interrelation between the *"physiogenic"* anxiety neurosis and the "psychogenic" psychoneurosis be hidden. The first patient temporarily lost all his psychic compulsion symptoms after he had experienced sexual gratification; with the return of sexual excitation, they recurred and lasted until the next occasion of gratification. The second patient, on the other hand, had meticulously worked through everything in the psychic realm, but in him, sexual excitation remained absent; the unconscious ideas at the root of his erective impotence had not been touched by the treatment.

Things began to take shape. I began to understand that an idea, endowed with a very small amount of energy, was capable of provoking an *increase* of excitation. The excitation thus provoked, in turn made the idea vivid and forceful. If the excitation subsided, the idea would collapse also. If, as is the case in the stasis neurosis, the idea of sexual intercourse does not arise in consciousness, due to moral inhibition, the excitation attaches itself to other ideas which are less subject to censorship. From this, I concluded: the stasis neurosis is a *somatic* disturbance, caused by sexual excitation which is misdirected because it is frustrated. However, *without a psychic inhibition, sexual energy can never become misdirected.* I was surprised that Freud had overlooked this fact. Once an inhibition has created the sexual stasis, this in turn may easily increase the inhibition and reactivate infantile ideas, which then take the place of normal ones. That is, infantile experiences which in themselves are in no way pathological, may, due to a present-day inhibition, become endowed with an excess of sexual energy. Once that has happened, they become urgent; being in conflict with adult psychic organization, they have to be kept down by repression. Thus, the chronic psychoneurosis, with its infantile sexual content, develops on the basis of a sexual inhibition which is conditioned by present-day circumstances and is apparently "harmless" at the outset. This is the nature of Freud's "regression to infantile mechanisms." All cases that I have treated showed this mechanism. If the neurosis had developed not in childhood, but at a later age, it was shown regularly that some "normal" inhibition or difficulty of the sexual life had created a stasis, and this in turn had reactivated infantile incestuous desires and sexual anxieties.

The next question was: Are the customary antisexual attitude and sexual inhibition which initiate every chronic neurosis "neurotic" or "normal"? Nobody discussed this question. The sexual inhibition, e.g., of a well-brought-up middle-class girl seemed to be considered as entirely a matter-of-course. I thought so myself, or rather, I just did not give any thought to the question. If a young, vivacious girl developed a neurosis in the course of her unsatisfying marriage, with cardiac anxiety, etc., nobody asked to know the reason for the inhibition which kept her from achieving sexual gratification *in spite of all*. As time went on, she would develop a full-fledged hysteria or compulsion neurosis. The first cause of the neurosis was the moral *inhibition*, its driving force the *unsatisfied sexual energy*.

The solution of many problems ramify from this point. There were, however, serious obstacles to the immediate and vigorous undertaking of such solutions. For seven years, I believed that I was working altogether as a Freudian. Nobody had any idea that these questions were the beginning of a dangerous mingling of basically imcompatible scientific views.

The "death instinct" [2]

Around 1925, there began a parting of the ways in psychoanalytic theory, of which its exponents were at first unaware, but which has become quite obvious by now.

. . . Reik had published a book on "Geständniszwang und Strafbedürfnis" [3] in which the whole original concept of the neurosis was made upside down. That the book was well received was so much the worse. Reduced to the simplest terms, his innovation consisted in the elimination of the concept that the child *fears* punishment for sexual behavior. Freud, in *Beyond the Pleasure Principle* and in *The Ego and the Id* had assumed the existence of an unconscious need for punishment; this was supposed to account for the resistance against getting well. At the same time, the concept of the "death instinct" was introduced. Freud assumed the living substance to be governed by two opposing instinctual forces: the life forces, which he equated with the sexual instinct ("Eros") and the "death instinct" ("Thanatos"). According to him "eros" would rouse the living substance out of its equilibrium, which is like the passivity of inorganic matter; it would create tension, would unite life into ever larger units. It was vigorous, turbulent and the cause of life's tumult. But behind it acted the mute, yet "much more momentous" death instinct; the tendency to reduce the living to the lifeless, to nothingness, to Nirvana. According to this concept, life really was nothing but a disturbance of eternal silence, of nothingness. In the neurosis, accordingly, these positive life

[2] *The Function of the Orgasm*, pp. 102-104.
[3] "Compulsion to Confess and Need for Punishment."

or sexual forces were opposed by the death instinct. Though the death instinct itself could not be perceived, it was argued, its manifestations were too obvious to be overlooked. Humans constantly showed *self-destructive tendencies*; the death instinct manifested itself in masochistic tendencies. These tendencies were at the bottom of the unconscious guilt feeling, which one might also call *need* for punishment. Patients simply did not want to get well because of this need for punishment which was satisfied in the neurosis.

It was only through Reik that I really found out where Freud began to err. Reik exaggerated and generalized many correct findings, such as the fact that criminals tend to give themselves away, or that to many people it is a relief to be able to confess a crime. Up to that time, a neurosis was considered to be the result of a conflict between sexuality and *fear* of punishment. Now, the formulation came to be that the neurosis was a conflict between sexuality and *need* for punishment, i.e., the direct opposite of the fear of punishment for sexual behavior. Such a formulation meant a complete liquidation of the psychoanalytic theory of the neuroses. It was in complete contradiction to all clinical insight. Clinical observation left no doubt of the correctness of Freud's original formulation: the patients had come to grief as a result of *their fear of punishment for sexual behavior*, and not as a result of any desire to be punished for it. True enough, many patients developed *secondarily* a masochistic attitude of wanting to be punished, of harming themselves or of clinging to their neurosis. But that was a secondary result—or a way out—of the complications into which they were driven by the inhibition of their sexuality. It was undoubtedly the task of the therapist to eliminate these desires for punishment as what they were, namely, *neurotic* formations, and to free the patient's sexuality; *not* to confirm these tendencies to self-injury as manifestations of deeper biological strivings. The adherents of the death instinct—who grew in numbers as well as dignity, because now they could talk of "Thanatos" instead of sexuality—ascribed the neurotic self-damaging tendency of a sick organism to a biological primary instinct of the living substance. From this, psychoanalysis has never recovered.

Reik was followed by Alexander. He examined some criminals and stated that quite generally crime is motivated by an unconscious need for punishment. He did not ask what was the origin of such unnatural behavior. He failed to mention the sociological basis of crime. Such formulations made any further thinking unnecessary. If one was not able to cure, the death instinct could be blamed. When people committed murder, it was in order to go to prison; when children stole, it was to obtain relief from a conscience that troubled them. I marvel today at the energy that was expended at that time on the discussion of such opinions. And yet, Freud had had something in mind which merited considerable effort in evaluating it; this I shall show later. However, inertia prevailed, and the labors of decades were lost. The patients' *"negative therapeutic reaction"* was later shown to be nothing but the result of theoretical and technical inability to establish orgastic potency in the patient, in other words, to handle their *pleasure anxiety*.

Lay analysis[4]

Until now, we have been concerned only with the question whether non-physicians should practice psychoanalysis on patients (analysis for therapeutic purposes). The problem has now been shifted insofar as Prof. Freud, in his book on lay analysis, has taken a further step, proposing to separate psychoanalysis, even in its medical aspects, from medicine; i.e., to train "a special class of therapists."

Let us now discuss his three most important arguments. Lay analysis, the practice of therapeutic analysis by non-physicians, is necessary:

1. Out of consideration for the application of psychoanalysis to the humanities.

2. Because it is feared that if its practical application were restricted to physicians, psychoanalysis could somehow sink into the insignificance of a mere chapter on "therapy" in some textbook on psychiatry.

3. Because the preparatory somatic training of physicians is secondary to psychological thinking.

To 1: It is said that non-medical analysts require practical experience in order to engage in scholarly pursuits. But the facts show that the application of psychoanalysis to the humanities is not advanced, but on the contrary suffers when its proponents become clinicians, too. The awakening clinical interest supplants all other concerns. The development of psychoanalysis in the humanities has ceased since lay persons have also been

[4] Excerpt from Reich's contribution to the symposium on "Lay Analysis" —1927.

practicing analysis. This argument is thus contradicted by experience.

To 2: The second argument reveals the deep distrust shown for psychoanalytic physicians, to the effect that with them theoretical interest and, with it, psychoanalysis as a science, would not be as well safeguarded as with the non-physicians because, allegedly, the former are more therapeutically inclined. The past does not justify this mistrust, and we do not want to decide about the future. At all events, psychoanalytic physicians do not seem to us to merit such distrust. In his discussion, Jones has emphasized the counterpart of this, namely Prof. Freud's exceedingly flattering opinion regarding lay analysts. Inasmuch as psychoanalytical psychology is so intimately related to the practical questions of everyday life that no step in the therapeutic sphere is possible without theory and vice versa, the theory must be as well guarded with physicians as with lay practitioners.

To 3: The third argument that the training of physicians "is practically the opposite of what is required as a preparation for psychoanalysis;" that, thus, somatic training is disadvantageous to psychoanalysis, likewise expresses the distrust of physicians qualitatively. And suddenly we see that the question whether lay persons should analyze alongside of physicians will be replaced by the other question whether physicians should analyze at all. Had Prof. Freud limited this criticism to the neurological concept of the neuroses, we would have agreed with him without any reservations. However, when we now oppose his authoritative opinion, we do so in the deep conviction of thus being of service to the cause of psychoanalysis. If psychoanalysis were in essence contrary to organic medicine, the following facts would be incomprehensible:

A physician discovered psychoanalysis. Most analysts, and not the worst ones, are physicians. Prof Freud once stated that psychoanalysis will one day be placed on its organic base. Furthermore—and, until now, this has merited much too little consideration in the question of lay analysis—he posited something somatic as the core of the neuroses and the essence of the affects. His concept of the libido means something physical (biological) as well as psychical. There are almost no patients without bodily symptoms or sexual disorders (disturbances of menstruation, potency, etc.). The analyst who is not organically trained is helpless in the face of the actual neurotic core of the neuroses, whether it concerns a vasoneurosis, neurasthenia or hypochondria.

On the other hand, we should like to assume with Jones that Prof. Freud has stressed so much the necessity of a "thorough" knowledge of theology and ethnology only in the interest of lay analysis.

Of course, we share Prof. Freud's opinion that the interest of science in this question must be decisive. However, it is precisely from this point of view that psychoanalysis cannot be too closely linked to medicine.

One need only consider the great area of the organic neuroses: hypochondria, neurasthenia and the psychoses. And do we not have much to expect from a psychology of the organic diseases? Or, after psychoanalysis has been separated from its foundation, must there be analysts who, as physicians, concern themselves only with the area bordering on the organic? In our opinion, neither science nor the patient would benefit by such a division. There would then continue to be doctors who know nothing of the psyche and psychoanalysts who are ignorant of the body. Moreover, a group of physicians would arise who would [only] be interested in the psychology of the body. The doctor would understand the analyst even less than he does today; and analysts, in turn, would completely forget that the "libido" has a somatic (endocrinological) root and a biological function. Surely it is not exaggerated to ask that everyone who wishes to treat the neuroses should be adequately trained in the conceptual content of the libido ("borderline concept between the psychic and the somatic").

The question of lay analysis is thus narrowed down factually to the extra-analytical preparatory training. At the present time, medical men offer the best guarantee of an adequate preliminary education. The fact that physicians have shown themselves so contemptuous and devoid of understanding toward psychoanalysis must be ascribed not to their somatic training but to their complexes. And have philosophers or biologists or academic psychologists who have come in contact with analysis behaved differently? Why is the "somatic prejudice" any more onerous than the philosophical one? Does not the philosopher always have the most complicated objections to analysis? With the analytically trained physician, the curse of somatic prejudice is at least compensated for by the blessing of natural-scientific and clinical thought. If medicine is caught in the meshes of mechanical-chemical thinking, then psychoanalysis is called upon to liberate it from its errors. One may condemn the medical man's complex-conditioned lack of understanding, but one need not, therefore, turn one's back on medicine. What speaks most in favor of the physician as therapist, even as a psychotherapist, is the fact that he has learned at the sickbed to deal with the sick and that brings along a measure of therapeutic interest which justifies study of the patient. I have heard lay analysts boast openly that they had no therapeutic interest. Why, then do they want to practice therapy?

. . . .

Expulsion from the International Psychoanalytical Association[5]

In the report of the Central Committee of the International Psychoanalytical Association (*Internat. Zeitschr. f. Psychoana.* 1935), a painful event is left out. For the orientation of the members of the Association, we complement the report as follows:

At the 13th International Psychoanalytic Congress (Lucerne, August 26 to 31, 1934), Wilhelm Reich was expelled from the International Psychoanalytical Association. This brought to an end the first stage of hard struggle, of eleven years' duration, for a correct natural-scientific psychology and theory of sex.

We cannot give here an extensive presentation of the motives behind this expulsion or of the differences within the psycho-analytic movement. This may be done at a time when further catastrophes in the scientific development of psychoanalysis, ca-tastrophes which are bound to come, will necessitate a detailed historical explanation. Here we shall show only briefly how con-servative scientific organizations of today fight workers who strive to take scientific research seriously.

The manner in which the expulsion of Wilhelm Reich took place is so grotesque as to appear incredible to the outsider. The

[5] First published in *Zeitschr. f. polit. Psychologie und Sexualökonomie*, Vol. 2 (1935), pp. 54-61. Translated by T. P. Wolfe, M.D. Walter Briehl, M.D., author of the chapter on Reich in the recently published *Psycho-analytic Pioneers*, perpetuates the myth that Reich "resigned" from the IPA. See footnote 2, page 8-9.

motive was nothing more than certain tactical considerations. Further, I don't understand what was hoped to be achieved by this measure, since I have announced a paper for the Congress and see no way of keeping myself hidden there from the German public. Provided, still, that it is only a matter of "certain" considerations, the fact that one did not choose the way of transferring me to another group, and the further fact that such things are done without my knowledge, behind my back, makes me think that something ominous is going on. To the world, the omission of my name must signify that I was either expelled or that I resigned. Since I have no intention of doing the latter, and since, to my knowledge, the former is not the case, the present attempt to solve the difficulty cannot be successful. I had occasion during the past year to show that I fully appreciate the embarrassment that I represent but that, for objective reasons, I cannot do anything to eliminate it. I would like to ask you, therefore, whether the omission of my name had the approval of the Executive Committee, and if so, the reasons for this measure, and the reason why I was not notified; it is also important for me to know what is the connection between this measure and my membership in the International Association.

I would like to ask you, at the same time, to let the Executive Committee know that I protest against this measure, and that I ask again that the present difficulties and moot questions be discussed, as usual, before the open forum of our members and readers. As painful as the circumstances may be, for everybody concerned, I must protest against being quietly put away in a corner. The problems with which we are all concerned and which are decisive for the future of psychoanalysis and its field of investigation need not fear the scrutiny of the world.

On August 8th, Reich received the following reply from Anna Freud:

Dear Dr. Reich:

The program of the Congress is on press and will be sent to the members within the next few days. In the meantime, you will have received the communication as to the place of your paper in the program.

Your complaint against the German Society I am referring to Dr. Jones. I did not know anything about the whole affair, and I am asking Jones whether he did. He will communicate with you directly.

On the eve of the Congress, Reich accidentally met a certain member of the Executive Committee in the lobby of the Congress building. This man told Reich privately that, a week previously, the German Psychoanalytic Society had decided on the expulsion of Reich, but that this expulsion was a "mere formality," since the recognition of the Scandinavian group was expected with certainty also to solve satisfactorily the problem of Reich's membership. Shortly afterwards Reich learned that the former president of the International Association and of the International Training Committee, Max Eitingon, had brought about Reich's expulsion from the German, and with that, from the International Association, *a year earlier*, in a *secret* meeting of the Executive Committee.[6] Of this, nobody had heard up to the time of the Congress. When the expulsion became known at the Congress, the members reacted in part with incredulity, in part with indignation, and in part with the consolation that

---

[6] *Translator's note:* After the publication of this article, Eitingon wrote to Reich, in a letter from Palestine, of December 29, 1935, that this statement was untrue, but that the contrary was true: "As late as 1933, when I was still in Germany, I was against your expulsion from the German Society and kept pointing out to the Executive Committee that under my aegis a thing like that would not be allowed to happen." In his reply of January 9, 1936, Reich stated that he was very glad to hear that Eitingon had no part in the action of the German Society against him; he regretted not to be able to correct publicly the presentation in the article as long as no public correction had been forthcoming from the administration of the Association; and that he would be glad to have Eitingon's letter published in the *Zeitschrift für polit. Psychologie und Sexualökonomie*, if he so wished. T. P. Wolfe, M.D.

the whole thing was merely a formality after all and that Reich would be admitted to the Scandinavian group. Nobody believed for a moment that the Executive Committee would confirm the expulsion. Very soon, however, it became obvious that it had been confirmed by the Executive Committee.

A decisive factor in the whole affair was the attitude of the Norwegians. The Executive Committee of the International Association tried to make the recognition of the Norwegian group contingent on their accepting the condition that they would not accept Reich as a member. The Norwegians, however, took the correct point of view: "We will not have conditions dictated to us. Make up your mind whether you want to recognize us or not. If you don't, we will resign." The decisive and upright attitude of the Norwegians (Hoel, Raknes, Schjelderup) made a great impression and intimidated the Executive Committee. They were recognized unconditionally as a group of the International Association; however, the Swedish group was separated from the Norwegian group, in order to remove it from Reich's influence. After his expulsion, Reich read his paper to the Congress as a guest.

It is not too much to say that the whole Congress was under the impress of this painful affair.

On the eve of the business meeting, in order to prevent a public scandal, a secret meeting was held of a representative of each of the local groups, under the chairmanship of Anna Freud, in order to "hear Reich's arguments." The whole thing was merely a gesture, for Reich's "arguments" were well known anyhow. He could only repeat there what he had said for years in his writings and in his correspondence with officials of the Association: He could not give in to the demand of the Executive Committee that he resign voluntarily. If the Executive

Committee expelled him, there was nothing he could do about it. He understood the expulsion from the point of view of the death-instinct theorists, for his own teachings had become so far different from the prevailing official teachings that there was no longer any common meeting ground. He declared himself, however, the most consistent and legitimate representative and developer of the original clinical and natural-scientific psycho-analysis, and stated that from this point of view he could not recognize his expulsion. He stated that, while this non-recognition on his part carried no organizational weight, he had to insist on the publication of the reasons for his expulsion in the official organ of the International Association. This was promised but not done. The later rumor that the Committee had "come to terms with Reich regarding his leaving the Association" only reflected the intense embarrassment caused to all those involved in it by the expulsion which had been decided a year previously.

. . . .

On Freud's eightieth birthday
Our congratulations to Freud
on his birthday (1936)[7]

By the time these lines reach the public, the noise of the celebrations will have subsided and the celebrants will wait for the ninetieth—and, we hope with them—for the hundredth birthday of Sigmund Freud to honor this man again. At that time, there will be a great many articles presenting the data from "The history of psychoanalysis" and from Freud's "Autobiography" to the public. Others, as at this time, will present the main

[7] First published in *Zeitschr. f. polit. Psychologie und Sexualökonomie*, Vol. 3, (1936), pp. 150-156. Translated by T. P. Wolfe, M.D.

features of Freud's theory and will talk, with more or less conviction, of its revolutionary character. All this is necessary and as it should be.

To us, these celebrations were food for serious thought. From what publications we have seen, it was abundantly clear that nowhere was the essential problem, "Freud and his environment," touched upon. It is as yet too early to present in detail the common fate shared by psychoanalysis between 1895 and 1920 and the young science of sex-economy, not to mention the even younger Sexpol movement. The event of Freud's eightieth birthday, however, should not pass without being correctly interpreted. It is necessary to point out what a whole world passed over in silence.

On May 6, 1926, the members of the Vienna Psychoanalytic Society celebrated Freud's seventieth birthday. There were many celebrants, flowers, and presents. Freud made a brief speech, which will remain unforgettable; nobody dared to make its contents publicly known. Freud warned that one should not let oneself be deceived, that all the praise proved nothing, that the world had not accepted psychoanalysis and continued to be inimical. A few years before, Freud had expressed the same feeling when he wrote that the world only accepted psychoanalysis, here and there, in order better to destroy it.

We fully agree with the point of view expressed by Freud on May 6, 1926. A look at the world and its important institutions shows us that things are worse today than they were ten years ago. We should not relinquish our watchfulness for a minute, for the fate suffered by psychoanalysis threatens our work a hundred times more severely. We experience now a phase of deadly silence on the part of the academic world and other influential circles. On the other hand, there are already signs of a method of benevolent destruction. Sex-economy is being represented as one of the deviations from psychoanalysis like that of Jung, Adler or Stekel. The reasons for this misrepresentation are stupidity as well as malice. He who knows the history of the psychoanalytic movement can see the difference at first glance. All deviations from Freud's theory, without exception, are characterized by the *negation* of sexuality. With Jung, the libido became a meaningless, mystical all-soul concept, the best possible soil for the later Gleichschaltung in the Third Reich. Adler replaced sexuality by the will to power, Rank denied the existence of infantile sexuality. Sex-economy, on the other hand, took its starting point precisely from those basic elements in Freud's theory which originally had aroused the ire of a world afraid of the truth. It developed the *orgasm theory* and tried in vain to incorporate it into psychoanalytic theory, where it organically belonged. It clarified the theory of the pregenital infantile sexual drives and built the basis for a characterology which has the sexual process as its core. Character-analytic technique required the full recognition of the laws of sexual economy. Many more things could be added to show why the theory of sex-economy inevitably begins to feel the previous fate of psychoanalysis. If it is to take itself seriously, it must do everything possible to avoid the fate which is overcoming psychoanalysis, no matter how noisy the sham praise of the world may be.

There is, today, nowhere in the world any official institution, pedagogical, psychiatric, or otherwise, which has made Freud's revolutionary concepts its own in a serious manner. Where is the mental hospital which systematically investigates the causation of mental diseases by the disturbance of early infantile *sex life?* Where is the academic institution which cultivates the rich treasure of analytic knowledge, engages in analytic research, and recognizes its full value? Where is the place where Freud's revolutionary knowledge finds its *concrete* expression? Who would, on the one hand, loudly proclaim his conviction of the magnitude of Freud's work and, on the other hand, take consolation in the fact that, after all, psychoanalysts have been given teaching posts at universities? Who believes that correct sexual theory could be taught in America of today? [8]

And what do things look like in the psychoanalytic movement itself? The English school is a sectarian circle completely divorced from life as it is. The Berlin Society attempted Gleichschaltung and thus perished. The Hungarian group consists almost exclusively of the house-analysts of rich people, without either scientific development or serious perspective. The Vienna Society is under the pressure of political reaction and ruled by some death-instinct theorists who no longer can be taken seriously from a scientific point of view. The French group looks desolate.

Has the socialist movement accepted psychoanalysis? Here and there *in words*, because political reaction placed Freud in the camp of Kulturbolschewismus. In the Soviet Union, psychoanalysis has been without development for years. There was ever so much talk about the significance of Freud for the workers' movement. Where, we must ask, has this significance become socialist practice? Nowhere. Socialists recommend to the workers the writings of reactionary psychoanalysts as guidebooks in "socialist psychology," such as an article by Roheim in a Hun-

[8] When I was about to start my lectures at the New School for Social Research in New York, in 1939, a psychiatrist and member of the Psychoanalytic Association advised me to keep off the sexual problem. Many things indicate that the sexual problem in its social functions is taboo. In spite of this, the prospects for sex-economy in the U.S.A. are good, provided that pornography is soon recognized and properly evaluated. Reich, 1946.

garian socialist periodical. Revolutionary socialists publish articles on the occasion of Freud's birthday but betray complete ignorance of the fierce struggle that has been going on for a decade within the psychoanalytic movement concerning the problem, "workers' movement and psychology."

The structure of Freudian theory contains contentions of very diverse kinds. Besides the theory of early infantile sexuality there is that of the "primary process" in the Unconscious; besides the theory of repression there is that of the death instinct; besides the theory of the determination of psychic processes there is that of "cultural repression," etc. The world asks for clarity. There are contentions which are indispensable, others which are non-essential, and still others which are only confusing. One would think that a scientific association which proclaims the world-historical significance of psychoanalysis would adhere to those elements of the theory which are basic, sound, and leading forward; but the opposite is the case. "Away from the main thing, we like the non-essential things," is the implicit slogan. It is most closely followed by some analysts calling themselves "socialists." They avoid "the main thing" like the pestilence; if they did not, they would find themselves, inevitably and immediately, in precisely that struggle which we lead and which they pass over in silence. They do everything they can to obliterate the front lines in the cultural struggle after they have been defined. They are as dangerous as the preachers of the objective spirit. They usurp findings and sabotage their meaning. It is necessary to warn against them.

The decline of the psychoanalytic movement, its adaptation to existing conditions, and the resulting sterility are not a matter for personal reproach. We have learned to pay attention to the dependence of science and its development on social processes.

Consequently, we profess a *socially conscious science*. We may say that we have taken into our care the revolutionary findings of Freud's theory. This makes it necessary to become clear in our minds about the existing situation and the factors which will determine the further course of our work.

The general world-political situation—in which we work with a theory of sex which is at variance with all existing institutions and official concepts—promises worse things to come. *This* world *cannot* acknowledge the fruits of our work or make use of them. It was we who were able to show what advantages political reaction derives from the irrational feeling and thinking of the masses, from their longing for happiness and simultaneous fear of sexuality. The diverse socialist parties are so bogged down in obsolete economistic thinking and so preoccupied with the tremendous problems of everyday that they cannot react differently towards us than with amazement or enmity. Nevertheless, much has been achieved in these difficult years. But what has been achieved is far from what is indispensable for the practical accomplishment of our tasks. Apart from the social difficulties, the most important factor inhibiting our work is our own structure.

Our psychological criticism of Freud began with the clinical finding that the unconscious inferno is not anything absolute, eternal, or unalterable, that a certain social situation and development has created the character structure of today and is thus perpetuated. We recognized that the fear of the "sexual chaos" is justified but also that it applies to definite historical periods; and our therapeutic work showed us that a different regulation of social living is possible. We have never entertained the illusion that the evil in man can be eliminated suddenly. We learned to recognize the enormous difficulties which a political psychology must expect if it attempts to bring about a real alteration of human structure. We ourselves, who have made this our goal, are only too often confronted with the weaknesses of our structure. It is not easy to master them, which is necessary if one is to be better equipped correctly to meet the effects of irrationalism in our fellow humans.

Psychoanalysis once worked at the roots of life. The fact that it did not become conscious of its social nature was the main factor in its catastrophic decline. From this, we drew the following conclusion: A science which has as its object of investigation life itself and which finds itself in a reactionary environment must either submit to this environment and relinquish its own principles, or it must organize itself, that is, create for itself the organs which safeguard its future.

Marxist economics was organized politically. In the realm of political economics, the political organization of science arouses no surprise. It is different in other fields. Here, the illusion of an "unpolitical science" has created much confusion. The science of human sexuality is in itself political, whether it wants to be or not; consequently, it must draw the conclusions and profess its social nature. From this, the necessity of organization follows. Then, the wealth of new knowledge is no longer at the mercy of this or that accident of social development, but is part of that political movement which has as its goal a rational, scientific guidance of society. No matter how concerned one may be with the irrational thinking within the socialist movement, natural-scientific psychology and correct sexology can have their place only within this movement.[9] Nobody will doubt this who has

[9] *Footnote, 1946:* This statement is no longer correct. The socialists, led by the communists, have in the meantime regressed sex-politically far behind the most primitive demands. Thus, social sex-economy finds itself in a great void, and its organization is left to future development. Reich.

followed the development of mysticism in Germany and its influence on natural-scientific research. We have no way of knowing today what forms the organization of our work will take in the broad masses of the population. But the necessity of creating a mass basis for it cannot be doubted. This not only will be a protection against reactionary influences from the outside but will also protect us against compromises with an inimical environment. If one is left without social influence, the environment will prove the stronger force. If, however, the people who count have understood the value of a scientific undertaking for their existence and their future, they will aid the struggle and diminish the pressure of an inimical outer world. Nobody can be absolutely sure of himself, ourselves included. If, during a favorable period, we stood out for, say, the necessity of a gratifying sex life in adolescence, a less favorable period may make us, nevertheless, give up such a contention or even denounce it. If, however, a sufficient number of adolescents have made our knowledge of puberty their own and are ready to defend it, we are spared such a retreat, and our scientific work is realized. This example may suffice to show what is meant here.

The social anchoring of our scientific work promises yet another gain. Freud started from physiology and discovered the nature of the psyche. Our criticism of psychoanalysis began with the *sociological* concepts of Freud. The consistent study of the interrelationships between the social and the psychic proved highly fruitful for clinical work also. There developed a basically new manner of studying the laws of sexual life. The orgasm theory, with an inner logic, led back to physiology and biology. The nature of the final results of this research cannot as yet be envisaged. The development is in full flux, the results are unaccustomed, the establishment of a biophysiological basis of psychology seems to succeed. We can already say that one of the most important of Freud's expectations is coming to be fulfilled: it will be possible to put the theory of psychic functioning on a solid biological basis. True, in a different manner than one had usually thought of.[1]

Thus, our obligation is twofold: that of safeguarding the practical realization of Freud's revolutionary achievements, and that of safeguarding our own sex-economic research. If we succeed in making the masses of working individuals who are deprived of their happiness understand what our work is about and why we have to struggle so hard, then, sooner or later, they will help us, will, as a social power, protect our work against outer and inner dangers and will themselves reap the fruits of the natural science about life.

No matter how difficult or hurtful the conflicts between psychoanalysis and sex-economy may have been, they will never cause us to forget what we owe to the life work of Freud. For nobody knows better than we, nobody experiences more painfully than we, why the world used to damn Freud and today removes him from a fighting reality.

[1] *Footnote, 1946:* This prediction was confirmed by the later development. It took the form of *orgone biophysics*, which developed into a new, fruitful branch of natural science. It owes its existence to the consistent adherence to the orgasm theory and orgasm research at which so many look askance. Reich.

Sex-economy and vegetotherapy in relation to psychoanalysis[2]

Sex-economy is the theory of the basic laws of sexuality. These basic laws are determined by the orgasm formula: tension→ charge→discharge→relaxation. Psychoanalysis is the doctrine of unconscious emotional life. Within the context of emotional functions there are certain relations to the psychoanalytic doctrine of the neuroses. The psychoanalytic doctrine of repression and resistance is carried further and becomes the sex-economic interpretation of the vegetative block. The basic psychoanalytic theory of the specifically sexual etiology of the neuroses is carried further and crystallizes into the sex-economic theory of the function of the orgasm, and of the resultant emotional disturbances if the orgastic function itself is disturbed. The psychoanalytic theory of determining conscious emotional processes by unconscious emotional processes is carried further and becomes the sex-economic theory of vegetative attitude and excitation.

These are the basic similarities, expanded into sex-economy, which are in harmony with the fundamentals of psychoanalysis.

Sex-economy is distinguished from psychoanalysis by the following factors:

The goal of psychoanalytic investigation is the discovery of unconscious emotional mechanisms. The goal of sex-economic investigation, supported by the character-analytic and vegetotherapeutic methods, is the discovery of vegetative physical mechanisms. The emphasis is on influencing the physical basis of emotional illness. This yields by-products which basically

[2] Elucidation occasioned by the Norwegian Government's Authorization of Psychoanalytic Practice (1938). Translated by Therese Pol.

confirm Freud's theory of the unconscious. The vegetative conditions of attitude and excitation which are released by the vegetotherapeutic technique invariably have a specific psychic content. The psychic content (a wish, an anxiety fantasy, an expectation, etc.) is not conscious to the patient. Among the meaningful psychic structures brought to light by vegetative excitation are most of the unconscious emotional ideas which psychoanalysis is accustomed to uncover with the interpretive method. A large number of unconscious mechanisms, such as the fear of bursting or the unconscious fear of orgasm, *cannot* be reached with the psychoanalytic technique of free association. Beyond this, the understanding of the physical attitude leads to an understanding of the form in which an emotional content is expressed. An anxiety fantasy can be inhibitive or agitating. Vegetotherapy has nothing to do with any kind of calisthenics or breathing exercises such as yoga. If anything, it is diametrically opposed to these methods. Calisthenics and all other breathing techniques are designed to teach the organism various movements or attitudes. Vegetotherapy strives to develop those attitudes, movements, excitations, and natural breathing rhythms that are specifically characteristic of the patient's personality.

The essence and goal of psychoanalytic therapy is to render unconscious material conscious by overcoming the emotional resistance to the awareness of the unconscious. The essence and goal of character-analytic vegetotherapy is to restore the biophysical equilibrium by releasing the orgastic potency; that is, not only to render unconscious material conscious, but to release vegetative energies.

The psychoanalytic goal consists in influencing the unconscious emotional content. For sex-economy, on the other hand, the therapeutic goal consists in influencing the disturbed sexual economy by restoring the ability to balance sexual energies. This is not done by influencing the unconscious emotional content and experience, but exclusively by influencing the form in which the emotional content is experienced.

Differences in technique:

The principal method of psychoanalytic therapy is "free association," i.e., essentially talking and communicating. The principal method of vegetotherapy consists in the disturbance of involuntary (hence unconscious) vegetative attitudes. Conversely, in vegetotherapy it is the not-talking—the elimination of conscious intensive oral expression—which is one of the principal methods for bringing to the fore vegetative feelings and affects, rooted in organic processes, *before* they become conscious.

Psychoanalysis avoids diagnostic judgments and influences on physical aspects traditionally associated with the medical profession.

In vegetotherapy the initial emphasis is on the physical, and not on the emotional, aspects. As a rule, the psychoanalyst sits behind the patient and, if possible, should not be seen by him. In vegetotherapy, this rule is suspended since it no longer relies on free association. Association of ideas has been replaced by the free unfolding of all vegetative attitudes—especially muscular action—characteristic of the patient.

Psychoanalysis is a psychology; sex-economy is sexology. "Sexology" is the science of the biological, physiological, emotional, and social processes of sexuality. Sex-economy is the first discipline to establish the profession of sex physician. Up to now this discipline was not taught as a specialized medical branch at the universities, and was practiced merely as a side line of other physicians such as gynecologists, specialists for venereal diseases, neurologists, psychoanalysts.

The abundance of emotional affects, which entail certain dangers in the hands of unskilled practitioners, requires an extremely tight control both in training and in practice. By definition, this control can only be exercised by specially schooled and experienced physicians and pedagogues. Hence the precondition for vegetotherapeutic practice differs fundamentally from that of psychoanalysis. The practice of vegetotherapy requires:

a) An adequate orientation in the fundamentals of sociology, i.e., of the laws of the social process which influence the strength of man's vegetative drives.

b) The knowledge of the basic elements governing the developmental history of sexual morality, from primitive society to the present state.

c) The knowledge of basic elements of psychiatry, with special consideration of the mechanisms operative in schizophrenia and in manic-depressive psychosis.

d) The work of the vegetotherapist demands precise knowledge of the autonomic or vegetative nervous system and the fundamentals of human physiology as well as endocrinology and sexual physiology.

e) A knowledge of the fundamentals of cell biology, vegetative current manifestations and electrical phenomena in protozoa are among the indispensable prerequisites for the practice of vegetotherapy.

f) Since vegetotherapy is increasingly penetrating the field of physical illness, knowledge of the relationship of the state of the [bio]-electric charge to the skin surface in neuroses and ego disturbances becomes a prerequisite of practical everyday work.

Sex-economy and vegetotherapy share only historical connections with psychoanalysis and meet together in the treatment of psychic processes in neurosis, but have progressed far beyond this point into the realms of *biology and sociology.*

Basic tenets on Red Fascism[3]

1. Communism in its present from as Red Fascism is not a political party like other political parties. It is politically and militarily armed *organized emotional plague.*

2. This organized political and armed emotional plague *uses* conspiracy and spying in all forms, in order to destroy human happiness. It is not, as is usually assumed, a political conspiracy to achieve certain rational social ends, as in 1918.

3. If you ask a liberal or a socialist or a Republican what he believes in socially, he will tell you frankly. The Red Fascist will not tell you what he is, who he is, what he wants. This proves that *hiding* is his basic characteristic. And only people who are hiding by way of their character constitution will operate in and for the Communist Party. It is *conspiracy and hiding for its own sake*, and not to use as a tool to achieve rational ends. To believe otherwise will only lead to disaster.

4. Red Fascism as a special form of the emotional plague, uses its basic characterological tool, hiding (*"conspiracy"*), "iron curtain," to exploit the identical emotionally sick attitudes in ordinary people. Thus the politically *organized emotional plague*

[3] *People in Trouble* (Orgone Institute Press, 1953), pp. 158-159.

uses the *unorganized emotional plague* to gratify its morbid needs. The political aims are secondary to this, and mostly subterfuges for emotionally biopathic activities. Proof: The political ends are shifted according to the "political," i.e., the emotional plague needs of hiding and causing trouble from ambush.

5. The hiding, conspiring, conniving are there *before* any political goals are conceived, as draperies for the activities.

6. The sole objective of the conspiring is *power* with no special social ends. The subjugation of people's lives is not intended, but is a necessary and an automatic result of the lack of rationality in the organization and existence of the emotional plague.

7. The organized emotional plague relies upon and uses consistently what is worst and lowest in human nature, while it slanders, destroys, and tries to put out of function all that threatens its existence, good or bad. A fact to the emotional plague is a fact only if it can be used to certain ends. It does not count on its own behalf, and there is, accordingly, no respect for facts. Truth is used only if it serves a special line of procedure or the general existence of the emotional dirtiness. It will be discarded as soon as it threatens or even contradicts such ends. Such an attitude toward fact and truth, history and human welfare is not specifically a characteristic of Red Fascism. It is typical of all politics. Red Fascism differs from other political disrespect for fact and truth in that it eliminates all checks and controls of the abuse of power and drives the nuisance politician to his utmost power. To believe that "peace negotiations" are meant as such is disastrous. They may and they may not be meant, according to the momentary expediency. Red Fascism is a power machine

using the principle of lie or truth, fact or distortion of fact, honesty or dishonesty, always to the end of conspiracy and abuse by human malignancy.

8. No one can ever hope to excel the pestilent character in lying and underhanded spying. Espionage and counter-espionage may belong as part of present-day social administration: It will never *solve* the problem of *social pathology*. Using *truth* in human affairs will burst open the trap and the unsolvable entanglement of spying and counter-spying. In addition, it will be constructive in establishing the foundation for life-positive human actions.

Truth versus Modju[4]

The pestilent character is usually a very active, mobile emotional structure; his mobility, however, is *short-circuited*, as it were, in such a manner that all splendid ideas and good intentions somehow evaporate before they can concentrate enough to produce lasting results. This is a serious work disturbance which gains importance through the fact that the pestilent character most likely will turn out to be an *"abortive genius."* The short-circuit in performance renders the great abilities abortive and frustrates the individual who suffers from this inhibited ability. Thus, he suffers from chronic frustration which, like all biopathies, is based on a deep disturbance of the function of full genital gratification (*"orgastic impotence"*). Since every truth will increase the frustration within the structure, the pestilent character must hate truth. Since he could basically, but cannot factually live

[4] Excerpt from the Orgone Energy Bulletin, Vol. IV, No. 3 (July 1952), pp. 166-170.

truth, he develops great ability in using the lie; not necessarily always the full, brutal lie, but most likely he will become a master in obtaining his goals by means other than open and frank procedure. Naturally, one will find all shades of lying, from the little innocent cheating in small matters to the BIG LIE of Hitlerian scope.

As a sexual cripple, the pestilent character who is endowed with more than average bio-energetic agility must develop channels to somehow live out his surplus energy. He will be a master in cunning, slyness, "know-how" in getting along with people *smoothly*. He will stand out little from the crowd. He will be a "good fellow," people will like him, he will appear honest and straight, and he will really mean what he says subjectively. But he will never quite overcome the feeling of being an abortive genius, gifted and crippled at the same time. This is strongly developed in him, and he has this trait in common with most average people. The people in general, however, have far less strained ambitions and are not as strong bio-energetically.

If, now, such a character joins a peaceful, hard-working group of people, he will smoothly fit in on the surface, but his inner frustration will sooner or later drive him to do underhanded mischief. Most spies who do not serve rational purposes probably are structured that way. To be hidden and to remain undetected has initially nothing whatsoever to do with the political or other kind of mischief. *The underhandedness is there earlier than the mischief.* It is the abortive genius, unable to accomplish lasting results, that drives the pestilent character to his underhanded actions on the public scene.

The pestilent character is basically a coward and he has much to hide, especially sexually. The hiddenness is essential to his social and emotional existence. It is safe to assume that such spies as Fuchs and others became fascist spies for dictators because fascism offers particular opportunities to integrate one's hidden character structure. It is clear that such pathological social phenomena as political movements which use and thrive on underhandedness are built on the foundations of such characters. It is clear from the history of the Russian Revolution why it was that a sly Djugashvili came to such power, riding high on the waves of the emotional plague. He shows all the character traits which characterize the pestilent character. But the riding to power and its misuse are not his fault or accomplishment. They are truly the result of the average character structure of multitudes of similar structures who feel incapable of the slowly grinding effort of lasting accomplishment, and, therefore, prefer the easy way of the politician who is obliged by nothing to prove his promises and contentions.

Djugashvili rides to power over millions, carried along by the very people whom he is going to suppress, supported and protected by what they have in common with him, be it ever so minute and little.

Let us briefly survey what public, pioneer, and administrator have in common with the pestilent character. Unless we find this common quality, we shall be unable to understand the great success of the emotional plague on the social scene; of the prevalence of the lie over the truth. No "congressional crime investigations" will ever change much on the social scene unless this point is brought to the fore and is understood. Otherwise, the actions of justice will only again hit the innocent, and lead to confusion and public panic. It is clear that the educator and psysician instead of the politician and policeman should be in charge of these affairs of social pathology.

Every living human being has something to hide—the pioneer, every soul that constitutes "the public," and every single public administrator. They have no big crimes to hide; these are little personal affairs which must be kept off the public scene, which is governed to such a large extent by gossip and character defamation. The core of this social anxiety always has been and will be for a long while the so-called "private life," or, put bluntly, the *love life* of the individual. Here an administrator has embraced a girl he knew in decency and honesty, but slightly out of range of what is considered "moral" by "the public." Many knew it, of course, but since everyone has such little and perfectly decent secrets, there is a common bond, so to speak, among the people who constitute what is called the public. Everybody has a more or less pressing bad conscience, well hidden under a mask of righteousness. Fear of getting into trouble with the law is quite general. Conformism stems from this fear and from these little secrets. And there is nothing whatsoever in the social set-up to understand, handle, or protect such innocent little secrets against invasion by dirty minds.

Sexual guilt feelings are quite general. Who has never touched his genital, or has never played around with a member of the opposite sex, or has not strayed off the path of marriage, and who has never committed a little crime here or there? Everybody has, of course, and we should feel very humanly about it, since one of the first things we do in fighting the plague is alleviate the severe pressure which is exerted upon the people by the false righteousness of politically ambitious district attorneys or senators, looking for "a case" or to further a career, or of policemen or politicians who find a ladder to peaks of power by way of nuisance investigations.

It is all right to stop rampant cheating in the realm of public lotteries, but one can see no harm in a little gambling or a little fun at pinball machines. It is the pestilent character again who here, too, spoils the fun for the people by misusing and abusing freedom of action.

Thus, everybody has something to hide. And it is this weak spot in everybody where our pestilent character sets in with his misdeeds. One can easily observe that the innocent public school teacher or social worker or mental-hygiene administrator will cringe before a letter written by a "tax-paying housewife" who protests against this or that. Only very few have the courage and the directness to step up and tell the public crank off.

The emotional plague has in a masterly fashion found a way of building its protective devices. Not only does it cunningly hook up with everyone's guilty conscience; it has put into circulation high-sounding ethical rules, which are perfect in themselves, such as: "One does not pay attention to such things as slander," or "It always has been that way and always will be," or "Every pioneer had to suffer." That something evil that "always has been" also has to be, is just as much empty talk as that of the "naturally suffering pioneer." The "liberal mind" has gone off the beam in a very bad way as far as such tolerance is concerned. It will soon become quite clear that under the cover of this protection enjoyed by the plague, innumerable murders have been committed, multitudes of decent adolescents have been delivered to penitentiaries or lunatic asylums, millions of innocent babies and children have suffered agonies and have been crippled for life, and, if we ultimately include the wars of humanity among the misdeeds of the well-hidden emotional plague, millions have died on the battle fields in vain, for MODJU only.

Thus, such slogans are more than empty. They are *murderous* talk, though innocently brought forth. However, this "innocence" itself will require clarification.

Those who talk that way mean it well. They are convinced of the ultimately decent nature of man. But, at the same time, they talk that way out of weakness and fear of the plague. They are factually hypnotized into immobility by the plague like a hen by the snake. Also, they certainly admire—at least some do so—the apparent toughness of the pestilent character, his suavity, his cunning, and his "know-how."

All this protects underhanded, manifold murder.

The mass of people are held down by fear of speaking up, by actual immobility of the emotional organism, by fear of trouble, by other serious worries, and by latent sexual guilt feelings. This renders them easy prey for the pestilent character.

They fall prey in spite of knowing the truth, of understanding the importance of bodily love, in spite of a sense of decency deeply ingrained but rendered helpless by so much cunning and conniving.

And the pioneering men or women often fall prey to the mischief because they are too busy, too honest, because they do not wish to soil their hands with the evil stuff.

And the administrator is dependent on public acclaim just as he is bound down as a human being by his own little secrets.

Now the pestilent character has easy going. He is protected on all sides and can proceed safely, without any danger of being detected, put into the bright sunlight, or challenged in any other way. If he adds political power machinery to his already rather well-set position he can conquer whole continents.

A little slander, well placed, excellently formulated, will, without great effort, kill many an important truth right away in its infancy or it will deprive it of social effectiveness if it had the strength to mature under such social pathology. The public will not act or render any help to the truth. It will remain *"sitting"* silently and watch helplessly or even gloatingly any crucifixion of innocent souls. The public administrator will be frightened to bits and try to maintain public morals and order. The pioneer will be silenced or he may go psychotic or fall into deep depression. Nobody is served except the pathological emotion of a nuisance biopath, MODJU again.

It is truly as ridiculous as that. However, behind this ridiculousness there waits for us a terrific problem of human existence:

HOW COULD SUCH RIDICULOUS NUISANCE GET INTO THIS WORLD IN THE FIRST PLACE, AND HOW COULD IT, UNDISTURBED, DEVASTATE HUMAN ORGANIZATIONS OF WORK AND PEACE FOR AGES?

However tough such problems may be to solve, we cannot ever expect to even start solving them unless we *free ourselves from the nuisance interference with serious human work exerted by the pestilent character.* It is necessary first to achieve a certain amount of safety in doing the job of finding answers to questions of living life.

A few successful procedures in stopping such interferences in the bud are the following:

1. Rely on the distinction between an honest and twisted facial expression.

2. Insist on everything being aboveboard.

3. Use the weapon of truth wisely but determinedly. The pestilent character is usually a coward and has nothing constructive to offer.

4. Meet the plague head on. Do not yield or appease. Master your guilt feelings and know your weak spots.

5. If necessary, reveal frankly your weak points, even your secrets. People will understand.

6. Help alleviate the pressure of human guilt feelings wherever you can, especially in sexual matters, the main domain of abuse by the emotional plague.

7. *Have your own motives, goals, methods always fully in the open, widely visible to everyone.*

8. Learn continuously how to meet the underhanded lie.

9. Channel all human interest toward important problems of life, especially the upbringing of infants.

There can be little doubt that the ravaging plague CAN be mastered, even easily, if the force of truth is used fully and without restraint. Truth is our potential ally even *within* the pestilent character. He, too, is somewhere decent deep down, though he may not know it.

Freud, Reich, Kinsey[5]

To prevent confusion, we must keep clearly in mind: Freud discovered *pregenital* sexuality in the infant and child to the first puberty. He touched upon genitality only in its *phallic* form in men and women (clitoral) alike. Genital functioning was to Freud "in the service of procreation" or else sublimated. There was no talk of genital or even orgastic satisfaction in the first and second puberty, the developmental stepping stones toward adult love activity in the biological sense of WR [Wilhelm Reich].

Kinsey and associates did not touch upon genitality in the sense of WR. They continued the line of thinking which derived

[5] From Reich's diary, October 15, 1953.

from the German and English sexologists of the end of the nineteenth century. These sexologists dealt with the *phallic-pornographic-clitoral* genitality of present-day man which has existed for some six to ten thousand years. They mistook and are still mistaking absence of vaginal genitality and the mere presence of circumscribed clitoral genitality as "normal" because it is characteristic of the majority of the female population. Accordingly, since clitoral genitality is a neurotic *substitute* for a blocked vaginal excitation, they confused the acme of the orgasm with the total orgasm which, in the orgonomic sense, includes, in addition to the acme, the ensuing convulsive movements. They thus confuse the present-day structure of genitality with the bio-energetic one, making the primordial life function, the orgasm, dependent upon nerve endings in the vagina. This view leaves no room for a comprehensive theory of genitality. According to the bio-energetic view of clinical orgonomy, the orgasm is identical with the total involuntary convulsion of the organism beginning with the acme (peak) of the orgasm and ending with complete relaxation. The orgasm function in the orgonomic sense reaches far beyond species and genus. It is older than the development of nerves. Its four-beat rhythm[6] characterizes cell division and the pulsatory movement of a jelly fish or the peristalsis of a worm or an intestine. It is clearly expressed in the protrusion of the pseudopodium of an ameba.

There can be no doubt about the basic bio-energetic function of the orgasm. However, from a biogenetic standpoint we may

---

[6] Known as the orgasm formula or "life formula," characterized by mechanical tension → bio-energetic charge → bio-energetic discharge → mechanical relaxation, observable not only in the orgasm, but in all the autonomic functions of the human organism; in unicellular as well as multicellular organisms; in the division of cells, etc.

consider whether a developed vaginal excitability exists throughout the animal kingdom, including the female of the human species, or whether we are moving in the female of man toward a *universal vaginal orgonotic functioning* as a further step in phylogenesis. Clitoral genitality would then only represent a first break out of the female genital from either *social suppression of genitality,* OR a primitive state of evolution.

Conclusion[7]

An immobilized, sitting humanity is waiting for an answer to its search for the ways of living Life. While it drudges along on a bare minimum of subsistence, waiting, dreaming, suffering agonies, submitting to new slaveries after ages of futile revolts, it is harassed by theories and dogmas on human living. To add a new dogma of human living to the maze of philosophies, religions, and political prescriptions means adding another piece of confusion to the building of the Tower of Babel. The task is not the construction of a new philosophy of life, but diversion of the attention from futile dogmas to the ONE basic question: WHY HAVE ALL DOGMAS OF HOW TO LIVE SO FAR FAILED?

The answer to this new kind of inquiry will not be an answer to the question of sitting humanity. However, it may open the way for *our children,* as yet unborn, to search in the *right* direction. They have over the ages long past, in the process of being born, carried all potentialities within themselves; and they still do. *The task is to divert the interest of a suffering humanity from unfounded prescriptions to* THE NEWBORN INFANT, THE

[7] *The Murder of Christ,* pp. 196-199.

ETERNAL "CHILD OF THE FUTURE." THE TASK IS TO SAFEGUARD ITS INBORN POTENTIALITIES TO FIND THE WAY. Thus the child, yet unborn, becomes the focus of attention. It is the common functioning principle of all humanity, past, present and future. It is, on account of its plasticity and endowment with rich natural potentialities, the only living hope that remains in this holocaust of human inferno. THE CHILD OF THE FUTURE AS THE CENTER OF HUMAN ATTENTION AND EFFORT IS THE LEVER WHICH WILL UNITE HUMANITY AGAIN INTO ONE SINGLE PEACEFUL COMMUNITY OF MEN, WOMEN AND THEIR OFFSPRING. In emotional power, as an object of love everywhere, regardless of nation, race, religion or class, it far surpasses any other interest of human striving. It will be the final victor and redeemer, in ways nobody can as yet predict.

This seems to be obvious to everyone. How is it possible, then, that nobody had as yet conceived the idea to center one's effort on this single hope and lever of true freedom, to unite man on this basis and to drain off his misdirected interest from futile, aimless, senseless, bloody convulsions?

The answer to this question was given: *Man lives and acts today according to thoughts which grew from the splitting up of the common stem of mankind into countless variations of thoughts which contradict each other. But the common root and stem of humanity remained the same: to have been born without ideas, theories, special interests, party programs, clothes, knowledge, ideals, ethics, sadism, criminal impulses; to have been born NAKED, just as the heavenly power has created it. This is the common root and stem of all humanity. Accordingly, it contains the common interest and power of unification of humanity. It is designed by the very condition of its emergence*

into the world to be beyond and above as well as at the founda-
tion of everything man thinks, acts, does, strives for and dies
for.

A brief survey may, in the end, show in what manner the kind
of thinking influences the use or the neglect of this common
root and stem:

The world of Red Fascism, thoroughly mechanistic in its economic system and perfectly mystical in its conduct of human
affairs, meets with human sitting on the spot and immobility,
badly equipped to do anything about it. It has, in sharp contradistinction to its spiritual founder, remained sitting on "economics" and a mechanistic, industrial view of society. It has
thrown out and kept away with fire and sword all knowledge
about human emotions ·beyond those known to the conscious
mind. It has condemned the bio-energetic drives as "bourgeois
ideology." It rests its philosophy of man on a merely conscious
mind which is superimposed on Pavlov's reflexes and automatic
responses. It has thrown out the function of love completely.
Accordingly, when it meets with human inertia, which is due to
the armoring of the biosystem, it believes, quite logically from
its own standpoint of thinking, that it is dealing with *conscious
spite* or *conscious* "reactionary" "*sabotage.*" Again, in full agreement with its way of thinking, and subjectively honestly (apart
from the conscious scoundrel of politics whom we find everywhere), the Red Fascist shoots to death the ."saboteur." This
must be so since, to this kind of thinking, what a man does or
does not do is due solely to conscious determination and resolve.
To believe otherwise, to accept the existence of a living domain
beyond the conscious will, and with it the existence and power
of an unconscious psychic domain, of a rigid character structure,
of an age-old impediment of bio-energetic functioning, would

right away and irretrievably undermine the very foundation of the total system of suppression of the "saboteur of the Power of the State." (Never mind now "proletarian" or otherwise.) It would, with one stroke, reveal MAN as he *is*, and the interest would be diverted from the "Capitalists" who are no more than ultimate results of an economy of armored, helpless, sitting mankind. It would reveal the truly capitalist character of Sovietism. The whole system of arch-reactionary oppression of living Life, of the total mess in the disguise of a "revolutionary" ambition, would inevitably collapse.

So much for the influence of thinking upon social action in terms of a "conscious mind" alone.

Let us now for a moment imagine that the psychoanalysts had acquired social power in some country. They would, from their point of view of the existence of an unconscious mind, acknowledge a vast domain of human existence *beyond* the conscious will. They would, if meeting with the "sitting" of humanity, attribute it to "bad" unconscious wishes of one kind or another. Their remedy would be to "make the spite conscious," to exterminate the evil unconscious. This, of course, would not help, just as it does not help in the treatment of a neurotic, since the spiting itself is the result of the total body armoring, and the "evil unconscious" is the result of the suppression of natural life in the infant; and "I won't" is superimposed upon a silent "I CAN'T." This immobility, expressed as an "I Can't," is naturally inaccessible to mere ideas or persuasion, since it is what orgone biophysics calls "STRUCTURAL," i.e., *frozen emotion*. In other words, it is an expression of the total being of the individual, *unalterable*, just as the shape of a grown tree is unalterable.

Thus, an emperor, basing his attempts to better the human lot on the making conscious of the unconscious and condemnation of the evil unconscious, would fail miserably. The unconscious mind is not the last thing and not the last word. It itself is an artificial result of much deeper processes, the suppression of Life in the newborn infant.

Orgonomy holds the view that human lethargy and sitting on the spot is the outer expression of the immobilization of the bio-energetic system, due to chronic armoring of the organism. The "I can't" appears as an "I won't," no matter whether conscious or unconscious. No conscious drill, no amount of making conscious of the unconscious can ever rock the massive blocking of man's will and action. It is, in the single individual, necessary to break the blocks, to let bio-energy stream freely again and thus to improve man's motility, which in turn will solve many problems arising from inertia in thinking and acting. But a basic immobility will remain. Character structure cannot basically be changed, just as a tree grown crooked cannot be made straight again.

Accordingly, the orgonomist will never aspire to break the blockings of life energy in the mass of humanity. *The attention will center consistently upon the newborn infants everywhere,* upon the infants who are born unarmored, mobile to the fullest. To prevent the immobilization of human functioning, and with it the spiting, the sitting on the spot for ages, the resistance to any kind of motion or innovation ("sabotage" in Red Fascist terms), becomes the basic task. It is the Emotional Plague of man, born from this very immobilization, which fights living, motile Life in the newborn infants and induces the armoring of the organism. *The worry is,* therefore, *the emotional plague,* and not the mobility of man.

This basic orientation precludes, naturally, any kind of political or ideological or merely psychological approach to human problems. *Nothing can change as long as man is armored*, since every misery stems from man's armoring and immobility which creates the fear of living, *motile* living. The orgonomic approach is neither political nor sociological alone; it is not psychological; it grew out of the criticism and correction of the psychological assumptions of psychoanalysis of an absolute unconscious, of the unconscious being the ultimate giveness in man, etc., and out of the introduction of bio-psychiatry into socio-economic thinking. It is BIOLOGICAL and BIOSOCIAL, resting on the discovery of the Cosmic Energy.

INDEX

LaVergne, TN USA
26 December 2010
210059LV00002B/64/A

9 780374 506728